PRE

The Story of
America's Greatest Running Legend
Steve Prefontaine

By Tom Jordan

D0036853

Rodale Press, Inc.
Emmaus, Pennsylvania

Distributed in the book trade by St. Martin's Press

6   8   10 9   7   paperback

OUR PURPOSE

*"We inspire and enable people to improve
their lives and the world around them."*

Contents

Acknowledgments

Pre is a book really written by dozens of people: those competitors and friends who willingly gave of their time and memories; the newsmen and their publications who kindly allowed me to reprint articles about Steve; the photographers whose superb photos capture the essence of the man. My heartfelt thanks goes to them.

In particular, I would like to thank Pat Tyson and Paul Geis for their candid observations and comments, and Kenn Hess, who graciously sent his personal files on Pre for my use. To Walt McClure, who provided Steve's high school career stats that appear in the Appendix, to Bill Dellinger, for his always-honest remembrances, and to Blaine Newnham, then the sports editor of *The* (Eugene) *Register-Guard*, who put me in contact with many of Pre's People through the pages of that fine newspaper. Thanks to Westcom Creative Group, for permission to quote from their compelling documentary, *Fire on the Track: The Steve Prefontaine Story*.

Thanks also to the superb staff at Rodale Press, especially Sara Dunphy, Eugenie Delaney, Andrew Brubaker, and David Umla. In particular, much gratitude goes to John Reeser, who edited the manuscript so adeptly and shepherded this project through so well.

Finally, thanks to Geoff Hollister, for his unselfish assistance; to *Track & Field News*, for enabling the story to be told; and to the Prefontaine family—parents Elfriede and Ray and sisters Linda and Neta, who have become a special part of my life.

Preface

Pre is primarily a chronicle of Steve Prefontaine's short, yet brilliant, career. Highlighted races are primarily from his track career. The track was his favorite venue, and he did his best running there. Some of his races, like the Olympic Trials and the Games, have been rediscovered by the media more than 20 years after his death in 1975; others, like his race against Hailu Ebba in the 1500 meters, are virtually unknown outside of Eugene, Oregon, his adopted hometown. There are cross country races included, because Pre enjoyed the fall program almost as much as he did track. A few significant indoor meets are covered, although Pre took the indoor campaigns less seriously than the other two seasons.

There are three inserts that contain many photos, taken by both amateur and professional photographers. These remarkable pictures hopefully relate what the text does not about Steve Prefontaine.

I would rather be ashes than dust!
I would rather that spark should burn out in a brilliant
blaze than it should be stilled by dry rot. I would
rather be a superb meteor, every atom of me in
magnificent glow, than a sleepy and permanent planet.
The proper function of man is to live, not to exist.
I shall not waste my days trying to prolong them.
I shall use my time.
    —*Jack London*

Introduction

There was something about Steve Prefontaine that demanded attention. As a writer for *Track & Field News* in the early 1970s, along with just about everyone else in the track world, I was fascinated by the phenomenon known as "Pre." His was a nature brash, fearless, outspoken, and—in the United States, at least—invincible on the track. To hear him hold forth to the media was to listen to a machine gun locked on automatic fire. To watch him back up his talk on the track was a thrill for his admirers and a frustration to his competitors. Either you were a Pre fan, or you were not. I was a fan.

My primary goal when I wrote this book in 1977 was to focus on Pre the runner and legend. During the writing, however, I soon found it impossible to speak of his career without including anecdotes about Pre the person. In interviewing Steve's teammates, competitors, fans, and friends, nearly all had a personal memory that for them typified Pre.

These memories two decades ago were given without prodding, sometimes eagerly, as if the grief could be mitigated by the sharing; sometimes in voices choked with emotion, poignantly reminding one that for those close to him, even two years after his death in 1975, it was but a yesterday ago. Indeed, many at the time still spoke of him in the present tense, saying, "Pre runs that third lap hard," or "Steve likes to wear purple a lot."

Nearly everyone described how Steve's life had affected

their own, at times told in terms too deeply personal for print. But other stories are included in the text; for without them, what would emerge is the Steve Prefontaine of the print media, a Pre who did exist, but only as one of the many personae he possessed. The fact of the matter is that each person knew a different Pre, witnessed a different side to this enormously complex individual. There were, to be sure, certain characteristics that recurred in any conversation about Steve with his friends and competitors. He was in constant motion, charged with an unbelievable energy. Yet in quiet moments, he was extremely easy to talk to. Pre would fix you with a steady gaze and give the impression that you were the most important person in his life at that instant, and that the things he was telling you were known by few others. It was an enormously flattering and appealing trait, and contributed greatly to what came to be called his "charisma."

At the same time, he was a hard person to know intimately. His pace was so frenetic, his outlook so taken up with the *now* of life, that his deep friendships outside of family and love relationships were few. And he was a private person, a loner at times, who "didn't like people butting in on his aloneness," as one friend put it.

"I didn't know him well," was a common refrain heard from those who were thought to be his friends in the track community. The very few who did become close to him saw a Steve Prefontaine different from the cocky, self-centered image found in the newspaper and magazine articles of the time. They saw a Pre capable of tears and self-doubt, of euphoria and thoughtfulness. They saw a "rube" from a small town fast maturing into an articulate adult, willing to take on the inequities he saw in the sport. Then, on a warm spring evening in late May, in a matter of minutes, his voice was silenced forever.

More than two decades have now passed since Pre's death, and his story is being rediscovered. A documentary on his life, *Fire on the Track*, was completed in 1995, and shown nationally on CBS before the live broadcast of the track meet bearing his name, the Prefontaine Classic. Astonishingly, not one, but two, major motion pictures are scheduled to be released in 1997, one by Disney and one by Warner Bros. The story behind the evolution of those two projects is worth a book in itself.

But why all the sudden interest in Pre? Why, after more than 20 years, all the attention on an athlete little known outside of track and field circles? Considering he never set a world record or won an Olympic medal, Pre's story could well be a mere footnote in the sport's history books. Some of his greatest races were at yard-distances that are no longer run. His rematch against Munich 5000- and 10,000-meter gold medalist Lasse Viren of Finland was going to be in the 1976 Games in Montreal. There, without Prefontaine, Viren won two more gold medals. Pre's opportunity for wealth and transcendent fame could well have come from the Running Boom, which only mushroomed in the late 1970s. In his lifetime, in fact, Pre never ran a serious road race.

So why all the attention on an athlete who, at age 24, was barely getting started in his running career and in life? The glib answer may be that those most affected by his life and death—his contemporaries—are now in positions to tell the stories they care to have told.

But a more accurate and compelling reason may be that there has come a realization that Pre's story is not simply one of a gifted athlete dying young. It is about an individual who in an incredibly short span of time helped instigate the end of amateurism, set the tone for a brash company that became the Nike colossus, and inspired generations of American distance runners by his complete commitment to wringing everything out of what he called "the Gift." Indeed, perhaps the most extraordinary aspect of the life and death of Steve Prefontaine is the number of forces his presence and subsequent absence set in motion.

And there is, for lack of a better term, the mystical element. It is astonishing the number of coincidences that relate back to Pre's life and death. Some are of the "how curious" variety, such as the sun always seeming to break through the clouds whenever he first stepped onto the Hayward Field track. Others are more macabre, such as Steve wearing a black singlet in a race for the first time in his career on the night he died, or one of the two torch bearers in the 1976 Montreal Olympics having the name—completely by coincidence—Stephen Prefontaine. Some, when told in the right circumstances, can almost make the neck hairs stand on end.

Among his many offtrack projects, Pre gave training advice and encouragement to two young women athletes with world-class potential. On May 30, 1976, one year to the day after Pre's death, Fran Sichting and her husband became the parents of their first child, a baby girl. On May 30, 1986, Mary Slaney and her husband became the parents of their first child, a baby girl. Runners are, by and large, a skeptical lot: It's hard to fool oneself during hard intervals or in the middle of a 10-mile run. But nearly everyone who knew Pre has a similar mystical story to tell. Just ask them.

1

Not Many Ways to Jump

Nothing hinted at what was to come.

Steve Roland Prefontaine was born on January 25, 1951, in the midst of the baby boom, in the Oregon coastal town of Coos Bay. He grew up with his parents and two sisters, Neta and Linda, in a snug house on Elrod Street built by his father. Ray Prefontaine had returned from serving with the U.S. Army occupation forces in Germany with his new bride, Elfriede. Both were hardworking, he as a carpenter and welder, she as a seamstress. They were a good fit for Coos Bay, where sloth was, and still is, a four-letter word.

Growing up, Steve was an active youngster, tearing around the house on his scooter, or after he grew older, setting speed records mowing the lawn. He would race HO-scale cars with his friends on Saturdays and go belly-boarding on Sunset Bay in the summers. His youth might have appeared unremarkable, even idyllic, but he was a product of his town and his time. Olympic marathoner and writer Kenny Moore explains it best:

"To understand Steve Prefontaine," he wrote in 1972, "it is necessary to know something about Coos Bay, Oregon. The town and the man find themselves similarly described: blunt, energetic, tough, aggressive. Coos Bay is a mill town, a fishing town, a deepwater port. Longshoremen, fishermen, and loggers are not given to quiet introspection. Coos Bay endures its difficult, elemental life in the woods, on the boats and docks with a vociferous pride. The working men insist on a hardness in their society. Youth must be initiated, must measure up.

"'You don't have many ways to jump,' says Prefontaine. 'You can be an athlete. Athletes are very, very big in Coos Bay. You can study, try to be an intellectual, but there aren't many of those. Or you can go drag the Gut in your lowered Chevy with a switchblade in your pocket.'"

Potential from an Early Age

Sports tradition runs deep in Coos Bay to this day. Perhaps because of its isolation, the small town of 15,000 invests much of its interest and enthusiasm in athletics. Football and basketball are especially popular, and the pressure to participate is intense.

At home football games during the 1950s and 1960s, a seemingly unending stream of 60 to 80 players, dressed in the silver-gray and purple uniforms of the Pirates of Marshfield High, would trot onto the field for pregame warm-ups, with the crowd standing and cheering. The varsity letter, notes a Marshfield grad who lived through the era, was "akin to a badge of manhood."

Colliding head-on with this ethic of toughness was an individual with something to prove. Years later, Steve would recall that he had been teased in grade school because of his hyperactivity, and because he was a slow learner. In junior high school, he tried hard to measure up. A 5-foot, 100-pound benchwarmer in the 8th grade, Steve—he wouldn't be called "Pre" until later—occasionally noticed members of the high school cross country team jogging by the football field on their way to practice.

"What kind of crazy nut would spend two or three hours a day just running?" was his reaction.

Pre's attitude changed that same year, during a three-week conditioning program in his physical education class. The longer the distance run, the closer he was to the leaders. He ran 3:51 for the 1320-yard run and 1:45 for the 660-yard run. "It somehow caught my interest," he said years later. Here was something he was good at, where determination coupled with talent could bring recognition and reward. Pre had found his sport.

He turned out for cross country in the fall of 1965 as a freshman at Marshfield High, and went from seventh man to second by season's end, placing 53rd in the state meet. His first year of track in the spring was less auspicious, with a 5:01 best in the mile.

"It was at the district cross country meet his sophomore year that his potential to become an outstanding runner showed itself," Walt McClure, his high school coach, states. "We were against the defending state mile champion and the boy who would become the state high school cross country champion, and there was maybe a quarter mile left to go when this little guy in purple passed them and took a short lead. They just went 'Who was that?' They got him in the end, and the same thing happened at the state meet, where he got sixth. Steve was really mad. 'Let's run it again!' he said, and he'd probably have beaten them if they had."

Now thoroughly hooked on running, Pre trained hard through the winter season and placed fifth in the Oregon Invitational, a showcase indoor meet for the best runners in the state, his sophomore year. His goals were high for the out-door track season, but months of frustration ended in his failure to make the state meet two-mile, caused in part perhaps by his strong interest in the performances of the other members of the team.

"He was always running up and down, shouting encouragement and advice," McClure recalls. "We finally had to tell him, 'Look, we'll do the coaching, you do the running.'"

Spurred on by his failure, Steve started planning for his junior-year cross country season with the goal of going unde-feated. He began to show the singular ability to accept mentally and physically the punishment of training.

"Pre was the hardest worker in running that I ever had by far," McClure remembers. "This is the whole thing, his intensity. On his morning runs, I didn't check on him. I just said if you want to be a good runner, you've got to get out there in the mornings.

"He asked, 'What should I do?' and I said you've got to be inventive, like sprint between telephone poles or just go out for 20 minutes and see how far you can go. He had a lot of imagination and thought of all sorts of things to do out there. He worked awful hard."

The intensity and hard work brought results. Gaps began to show between Pre and the pack, and there were no more incidents like the one during his sophomore year, when in a physical cross country race against Sheldon High School, the tough kid from Coos Bay indelicately took a swing at rival Jon Anderson, the future winner of the 1973 Boston Marathon.

Pre went undefeated in cross country his junior year, culminating in the state title. Bill Dellinger, University of Oregon assistant cross country and track coach at that time, remembers his first glimpse of Pre at that meet. "I was standing on a hill. I had my binoculars, and I was probably a good half-mile or 700 yards away from the start. And I saw this guy that had the start position, but it was the look in his eyes, from a half-mile distance, the intensity in his face as the gun went off. I thought, 'That's got to be Pre.'"

Outdoors, the 17-year-old prodigy set an all-time Oregon track best in the two-mile with a 9:01.3. He trained everywhere, on the beaches and dunes, and on the golf course where the team did some of its training.

And at all hours. After being stopped a couple of times by the police inquiring about just exactly what he was doing, Steve was left alone.

"He was a little bit ahead of his time in Coos Bay," chuckles McClure. "It was kind of comical to hear some of his comments about being stopped."

Besides the four to eight miles a day, Steve's enormous energy was spread between three part-time jobs: working as a gas jockey in a Phillips 66 station, as a water-safety instructor, and as a policy evaluator for a local insurance company. He also listed his hobbies on a *Track & Field News* questionnaire as "water skiing, sand buggy riding, stamp collecting, [and] drawing."

The overwhelming impression for the residents of Coos Bay, however, was of Prefontaine, the kid who never stopped running.

"I used to see Pre training while on my way to work," a

longtime Coos Bay resident recalls. "He used to run through Mingus Park, past the swimming pool and then up the steep Tenth Street hill and beyond. It's an odd thing, but although I saw him running the streets and trails of Coos Bay about a hundred times, I don't think I ever saw him running downhill. Seems like he was always going up."

Pre started to feel that special responsibility to his roots and "his people" that was to hallmark his career in both Coos Bay and Eugene, at the University of Oregon. On his morning runs, toward North Bend up the highway, he shared an affinity with other early toilers. "A couple of guys I know who wave at me," he said. "Some of the bread men, garbage men, and street cleaners."

"I Want to Be Number One"

Pirate Stadium began to fill for track meets, and Steve gave them a show, though he didn't run any victory laps while at Marshfield. He drew the fans, partly because they wanted to follow the fortunes of this lad who was never satisfied, and partly because they sensed that Pre was something special.

"A lady came into the store where I worked," Steve's mother remembers, "and said, 'Mrs. Prefontaine, you should go to the meets. Your son is Olympic stuff.' I still remember the words."

"What I want to be is to be number one," is how Pre so aptly put it.

Senior year began with an easy defense of his cross country title and aggressive goals for a 9:00 two-miler. He wanted by the end of his senior year to run a 1:52 half-mile, a 3:56 mile, and an 8:40 two-mile. McClure set the workouts with those goals in mind, and the early ones, at times, Pre could not finish. But he drove himself relentlessly.

"His talent was not that he had great style," McClure assesses. "He didn't. It got better I think. We worked probably harder on that than we did on anything. He'd like to slump over, and we'd keep hollering at him. No, his talent was his control of his fatigue and his pain. His threshold was different than most of us, whether it was inborn or he developed it himself."

"What I like most about track," Pre said at the time, "is the feeling I get inside after a good run."

To achieve their ambitious goals, Prefontaine and McClure had to battle the late Oregon spring, rival runners, and a high school dual-meet schedule offering few opportunities for all-out assaults on records.

Following McClure's orders in the early meets, Pre went hard only one race per meet, running a 4:11.1 mile and a 9:13.4 two-mile one week, and a 4:19.4 mile and 1:54.3 half-mile the next. But by the end of April, Pre was ready to tackle the most important of his goals, at the Corvallis Invitational: the national high school two-mile record of 8:48.4 held by Rick Riley.

The plan was for the first mile to be in 4:24 and the second in 4:20.0. That would yield a time well under the record, and put Pre within 8:40 range at the state meet a month later. On the Monday before the Invitational, Steve had run four half-miles between 2:07 and 2:10, with a 110-yard jog in between each one. "It came out to be an 8:36 two-mile," he said. "After that, I was ready."

It was a night meet, and a chilly one. Despite his outward confidence, Pre approached McClure before the race and said that his stomach had been upside down for three days. "I told him mine had been that way for five weeks," McClure notes. "The last comment I made to him, and this was because he was so intense that he sometimes ran the first part too fast, was 'if you're wrong on pace, be slow.' So he ran a 69 on the first quarter-mile."

"My first lap was too slow," Pre said, a month after his record, "but I knew I couldn't make it up all in one lap. So I went to work on a 66-second pace per quarter-mile after the first mile. I thought I better go to work. I hit the last lap and I knew I had it, so I opened up a little. My last lap was 61.5, and my second mile felt better than my first. I think I should have started my kick sooner." His time was 8:41.5, 6.9 seconds better than the old record.

"After I heard my time, I wasn't tired at all. I felt on top of the world."

With the first goal accomplished, the district and state

meets were the next venues for fast races. But Marshfield was in the team race for the state title, and Steve willingly sacrificed record attempts in one event so that he could win both the mile and two-mile races. "We weren't going to run his guts out," McClure says of their strategy. But other runners had different ideas.

Doug Crooks of North Eugene pushed Steve to the tape in the district mile, a tenth of a second behind Steve's 4:07.4. And Mark Hiefield of Milwaukie set a strong pace throughout the state two-mile before Pre opened up a small lead on the backstretch of the last lap and held it for a 9:03.0 win. Winning the mile and two-mile races at both meets was unprecedented in Oregon, and the sacrifice of further record attempts seemed a tolerable price to pay.

All during that successful senior season, the flood of phone calls and letters recruiting Steve to this school or that increased as the time for making a decision drew near. Steve directed most of these to his coach, and McClure made short work of the latecomers. Also, in his heart, Walt wanted Pre to go to the University of Oregon, his alma mater. Steve was pretty sure he wanted to go there or to Oregon State, but he hadn't heard anything from University of Oregon cross country and track coach Bill Bowerman. Bowerman was the legendary coach of a succession of world- and American-record holders, including Bill Dellinger and Dyrol Burleson, who, like Pre, grew up in small Oregon towns.

"Then I got a handwritten note," Pre said. "I could barely read it. It said if I came to Oregon, he'd make me into the best distance runner ever. That was all I needed to hear."

Bowerman doesn't remember it quite that way. "I recruited Steve the same way I recruited everybody," he says emphatically. "After all, the athlete makes himself, the coach doesn't make the athlete." But Bowerman had been following Pre's career since he was a high school sophomore, and had agreed with McClure's statement that "Here's a little guy who's pretty good." He agreed so much that he wrote a letter to the community of Coos Bay after Steve chose the university, thanking them for their part in Steve's success thus far.

"I have every confidence," he wrote, "that if he keeps his eye on the target, and his dedication, with his background and with the future, he will become the greatest runner in the world."

Pre and Oregon had chosen each other. And with a win in the mile at the Golden West Invitational, an all-star meet in Sacramento, California, featuring some of the country's best high school athletes, Pre's Marshfield career was over. Fittingly, he won in a personal best of 4:06.0.

Almost immediately, he made the plunge into world-class competition.

International Competitor

The 1969 Amateur Athletic Union (AAU) Championships were to be held in Miami at the end of June, and the people of Coos Bay opened their pocketbooks to send their favorite son to run the three-mile. The AAU governed the sport of track and field at that time, and its annual national championships determined who would be selected to run for the United States in international competitions. All of America's best distance runners would be there, including much older and stronger postcollegiate athletes.

Pre was game. The three-mile distance was one, in McClure's words, "we weren't quite ready for," but you wouldn't have known it watching the race unfold on the hot synthetic surface of Miami-Dade South College.

Former high school great Gerry Lindgren and Olympic veteran Tracy Smith quickly broke away from the pack and kept it a two-man struggle for first place. Back in the pack, Steve moved from seventh to fifth, then charged home on the last lap for fourth and a spot on the AAU team.

Steve was drafted into early service when second-placer Smith chose to run in the Military Championships in France instead of the U.S.-U.S.S.R.-Commonwealth meet in Los Angeles in mid-July. Jerry Uhrhammer of *The Register-Guard* in Eugene got hold of Steve in Coos Bay with the news. "Pre had just returned from his second workout of the morning when he answered the telephone, still breathless.

'I haven't heard anything (pant, pant) about it,' he gasped.

'All I know is that I've got an airline ticket for Hawaii (pant, pant).'"

As part of the overall team preparation for the summer's meets, the U.S. team and alternates (Pre was one) went over to Honolulu for some training and racing. Pre was looking forward to challenging the Russians when the AAU informed him just two days before the race that Smith had decided to run in the Los Angeles meet after all. Pre was not pleased. "So now I have to sit on the bench when I was really ready to run a good, or the best, race of my life," he groused.

Then, in yet another turnabout the day before the race, and after completing a hard workout, Steve was told by AAU officials that Smith had withdrawn because of illness. Thus began a deep-seated dissatisfaction with an organization he continually found to be autocratic, unresponsive, and out of touch.

A chagrined Pre was teamed with Lindgren in the 5000 meters. He stuck closely to pacesetter Lindgren for the first mile of his first international race. The crowd of 15,000 cheered on the high school kid, but he gradually lost touch with the pack and faded to fifth and a creditable 14:40.0.

Next, the 18-year-old from Coos Bay was on his way to Europe with the AAU team for three meets. While in Europe, he wrote a series of letters to Kenn Hess, then with the *Coos Bay World* newspaper. Pre was a prodigious letter writer, if at times somewhat unorthodox. "Steve spoke better than he wrote," says a friend, "because he was always in too much of a hurry to punctuate his sentences or read over for errors. In fact, I'm surprised he had the patience to write at all." One of Pre's letters from West Germany tells of his progress during the summer.

Augsburg, W.G., Aug. 2, 1969
Well I didn't get first but I didn't get last either. Thats the way I should of run in Los Angeles, and in Miami. I knew I had it in me but I had to prove it to myself. Now I'm ready to run with anybody cause I know what I can take I'll just have to polish up on my form which was not the best but not bad either. I was

relaxed the whole race except for the last lap and I got stiff again and couldn't go when Jerry and the other guy took off.

Here is how the race went the first lap was about 62, then for the 800 meters it was 2:05.3, 1500 meters 3:58.0, for the mile 4:13 to 4:14 the 3000 meter mark was in 8:07.0 and the two mile mark was in 8:42 something, the three mile mark was about 13:20 maybe a little faster maybe a little slower and then I came home with a 13:52.8 my last lap was not to good no sprint left.

Now we're in Augsburg, what an old city the houses here are hundreds of years old, the people here are very friendly, we all went to a old fashion party last night they had the band and the dancers and the big lieter beer mugs, which are just huge. I had one and that was enough for me. They gave us two for present to take home.

Well I best go I've got a meeting to make tell Walt hello for me.

Yours Truly, Pre

This first international tour had been instructive. He had finished third in the 5000 at the United States versus Europe meet, and his 13:52.8 time was faster than any ever run by the legend of the previous generation, Emil Zatopek of Czechoslovakia. Pre had found that he could hold his own against the world's best. That fall, as he left Coos Bay for the college town of Eugene, Oregon, Steve felt ready to take on all comers.

"He was self-confident, yes, sir," McClure recalls of the Pre of 1969. "He wasn't cocky, as a lot of people accused him of later. He had a lot of pride, but it was constructive. Evidently, he had problems with the press or something. If you ask dumb questions, you get dumb answers, I guess.

"I was just a short period in that guy's life, but he kept in contact with me no matter where he went. That's not the nature of some guy who does everything on his own."

2

The Rube

Most freshmen enter college with only a vague idea of what they want to pursue as a vocation. Steve thought that he would like to major in something that would lead to a career in "insurance work or interior decorating." That he eventually majored in Broadcast Communications shows the range of Pre's interests. As an 18-year-old self-styled "hick" from Coos Bay, he was just brash enough to think that he could do anything he put his mind to, on the track or off.

"He was just pretty naive as a freshman," reflects Bill Dellinger, who took over as head cross country and track coach after the retirement of Bill Bowerman in 1973. "He was someone who didn't know any better and went out and did whatever he said he was going to do. We nicknamed him 'The Rube.'"

There was no identity crisis shadowing the personality of Steve Prefontaine. Take the time he and a friend went into a Eugene sporting goods store and the clerk asked if they knew anything about the good runner from Coos Bay. Steve unabashedly said, "Hey, that's me, and it's pronounced 'Pre-fon-taine.'"

Another freshman entering at the same time was Mac Wilkins, who would go on to win the gold medal in the discus in the 1976 Olympic Games.

"Pre lived right across the hall from me in the freshman dorm. Unfortunately, his room faced in on the dorm complex, so there weren't a lot of people who could see his bedroom window. But he still managed to hang his USA sweats up there, with the 'USA' facing out. That first year in school, he had a 1956 light blue Chevy with the back end jacked up, mag wheels, and fur on the back under the window—that was his car!"

There was a defensiveness underneath Pre's show of self-confidence, however, which may explain some of his swagger. "When I first met him," Mary Marckx, a close friend and confidante, remembers, "he had a great deal of difficulty around campus. Oregon was very anti-athlete at the time, just after the 1960s. Steve was kind of an arrogant person anyway, and when he first started college, I don't think he related too well to people; he thought they were prejudging him. Plus, he used to get nasty letters and notes on his door, crank calls—he was really harassed a lot. He built up his own little defense for awhile. As time went on, he just kind of grew out of it."

Part of that defense was his Coos Bay toughness, in which he reveled. It came in handy in workouts, especially, where Pre challenged the best runners of a school known for its distance runners. Pat Tyson, who was to become Steve's friend and roommate, recollects the feeling of team members toward the prodigy.

"Some were kind of envious, you might say, yet at the same time thought it was neat having him there. But that's the way it was at Oregon: You're friends, but when you're on the track, you're there to beat somebody else out. Steve was kind of above that, though, because even as a freshman, he was at national caliber."

Or better. During the dual-meet season, Pre was unbeat-able. As the season progressed, he challenged more aggressively than ever, beating Washington State's Gerry Lindgren, his AAU teammate from the previous summer, in the Pac-8 Northern Division cross country meet at Oregon State, when Pre chose to wear spikes over the muddy terrain, and Gerry went with flats.

Lindgren came back, and in the Pac-8 cross country meet at Stanford, he clung to Prefontaine through a brutal 4:23 first mile. Leaving the pack behind, the pair strove purposefully for five miles, giving the impression that a struggle for collegiate distance dominance was under way.

"We took off together," Lindgren says, "and we were never more than eight yards apart during the whole race. I'd try to shake him, and then he'd try to shake me. Neither of us could take command."

Then, during the sixth, and final, mile, they talked. Up the finish straight to the tape, the gut-wrenching drive of which they were both capable was missing. Lindgren was awarded the victory. Both scoffed at talk of an intentional tie. "I didn't know I had it won until later," Lindgren said.

"It was that close," Pre added. "I was going all out. We didn't plan to tie."

The National Collegiate Athletic Association (NCAA) cross country championships were in New York City that year, and Prefontaine took the last defeat in a cross country race of his career. Lindgren, overcoming nagging injuries, and Mike Ryan, the defending champion from Air Force, finished ahead of Pre.

"I was scared, really scared," Lindgren said, "so I wanted to lead all the way."

Pre had what was to be a rarity for him: an off-day. "I don't know what happened," Pre shrugged. "I like a fast pace, but I just wasn't right today."

Ready for All Comers

A brief, successful indoor track season merged into the wet spring of 1970. As was customary for many northern schools, Oregon's track team traveled south to California and Texas in March and April for a series of dual and invitational meets. Pre's success at these meets prepared him for his first three-mile ever in Eugene, a dual meet against Washington State.

A head cold left him stopped up, and the rain and raw wind at the University of Oregon's Hayward Field in late April were not particularly inviting. But Pre ran a 4:17 first mile, far faster than the planned 4:30 pace. "My rhythm was going good," he would say afterward, "and I thought, 'I'm not slowing down to 9-minute pace now!'" He passed two miles in 8:45 and finished three miles in 13:12.8, seventh-fastest ever by an American and the fastest time by a U.S. runner in two years.

"I felt like I should have made my sprint earlier," he said, in what was to become a familiar refrain. As hard as Pre raced, he always thought that he could have gone faster if there had been someone to push him. "They say you get stronger as you get older," he continued. "If I keep getting this much stronger every year, I don't know what I'll be doing. Plus I feel faster and more confident."

Pre cruised through that first year of track, easily winning the three-mile at each meet through the Pac-8 Championships. By the NCAA Championship meet in June, Steve could hardly have been more confident. He had run a mile 15 days before in 3:57.4, a personal best by three seconds. It was also one of only three races—all miles—that he ever lost in Eugene. Oregon teammate Roscoe Divine edged him out with a 3:56.3. But Pre was satisfied with his personal record. He felt ready for all comers in the three-mile at Des Moines.

"I think the first time I met him personally was my freshman year," rival Garry Bjorklund of the University of Minnesota recollects. "He scared the pants off me. Pre was the first person I met where there was so much to bite off, you couldn't chew." Bjorklund, too, was a freshman, and his 4:05.1 high school mile time the year before had been the only one in the country better than Pre's 4:06.0.

Bjorklund and Villanova's Dick Buerkle challenged Pre with two laps to go, but he fought them off despite a painful gash on his right foot from an altercation with a diving board bolt three days before. Twelve stitches and 24 hours in ice got him to the starting line; toughness brought him the win in 13:22.0.

"I haven't looked at it yet," he grimaced after the race. "I'm kinda scared to look at it."

Despite his injury, Pre had run his last half-mile in 2:00.4, scotching rumors that he had no kick. Indeed, before the AAU meet in Bakersfield, California, a week later, he boasted to opponent Rick Riley of Washington State, "I ran a two-minute half in the NCAA, and nobody—nobody—is going to outsprint me!"

But on a frantic last lap at the AAU three-mile race, first Frank Shorter, a postcollegian running for the Florida Track

Club, then Riley, then Lindgren, and finally Jack Bacheler, also running for the Florida Track Club, cruised by the Oregon freshman. He had run 57.8 for the last lap, but it hadn't been good enough. He did manage to nose out Bjorklund, however, in a manner Garry recalls with humor.

"At that time, I still thought of myself to be a bit of a kicker. On the last lap, Pre got a jump on me and I closed again and again, and on the corner, I went to go around him . . . and he went out with me! I lost stride and never caught him to the finish. I had him that day, I think, but when you come from northern Minnesota, you don't see those tactics very often."

The fifth-place finish qualified Pre for his second AAU tour overseas. In the first match against West Germany, Steve first met the runner he perhaps liked least as an opponent—Harald Norpoth.

For 4750 of the 5000 meters, Prefontaine led, with Norpoth shadowing, and teammate Kenny Moore and Werner Girke of West Germany dropping back. On the last lap, the 26-year-old Norpoth unleashed a potent kick and won going away in 13:34.6.

Pre was disgusted.

"I don't have respect for a runner who'd let a kid do all the work and then go by at the end," he grumbled. His evaluation was typical. He was the 19-year-old "kid" pitted against "old men." He had time yet, to grow and mature, to become better. It was an attitude stemming probably from something that Coach McClure had tried to teach him before he left Marshfield High.

"My one concern was that he understand that his accomplishments as a prep runner were just a beginning, a plateau from which to reach future greater heights. 'Don't peak out after high school, or I will have disserved you,' was my plea. He assumed this responsibility in typical fashion."

"Never Give a Inch"

Back in Eugene, the international veteran tried to make ends meet. The fraternity he had moved into in the fall of his sophomore year went under and was converted to Mama's, a natural foods eatery. Pre had served as the fraternity's breakfast cook—up at 6:00 A.M., out for a 30-minute run, then in to cook breakfast before classes.

Amid this impossible schedule, he went undefeated in cross country, including his first of three NCAA cross country titles when he broke the field assembled at Williamsburg, Virginia.

On the track, he dominated early-season meets, and the collegiate supremacy he had displayed in 1970 continued into 1971. By the Pac-8 meet in Seattle in May, he had a string of 21 straight collegiate meets without a loss. He was the hotshot prodigy, on the cover of *Sports Illustrated* as a freshman, and his fame still growing as a sophomore. He was called "World" by his teammates, a nickname Mac Wilkins came up with to keep Pre humble. It was short for "World Famous" and Pre disliked the name so intensely that Wilkins was the only one who dared use it to his face with any regularity.

From the public, there was adulation, which Pre, depending on his mood, either catered to or disdained. On the one hand, Steve proudly clipped all the news stories about himself and pasted them into a scrapbook; but he could also be hard on those he suspected of sycophancy, and he protected his privacy when possible.

At the Pac-8 meet in Seattle, Washington high school miler Scott Daggatt had his first encounter with Pre. "I saw this guy in dark glasses, and I knew it was Prefontaine. I said, 'Are you Steve Prefontaine?' and he said, 'No.'

"I go, 'Are you a distance runner?' and he says, 'No.'

"I said, 'I really don't care who I talk to. I just want to know a little about Oregon. My name is Scott Daggatt and I'm thinking of going there.'

"Then he introduced himself as Steve Prefontaine."

By this meet, too, Pre's reputation for invincibility in stateside distance running was formidable. The fact of his toughness had an effect on other distance runners.

Don Kardong of Stanford, a talented runner and more mature by three years, writes of what it was like to race the young Prefontaine.

"A strange camaraderie grew up at the time among those of us who lost continually to Pre. It was like the unity of the townspeople in Ken Kesey's novel *Sometimes a Great Notion*, a feeling grown of inadequacy and envy of a man whose motto, in Kesey's words, might have been, 'never give a inch.' We were united in our belief that no one should have the success coupled with pride that Pre had. We really wanted, I think, to see the big tree fall.

"The Pac-8 in Seattle opened my eyes. Admittedly, he had already won the mile, but the feeling still seeped into my consciousness. I could run with Pre. I could slipstream him. I might not beat him, but even in losing I was following his path to the top.

"With about a mile left in the race, Pre passed me. Pride grabbed me, and I took the lead back. I tried to press hard, to be the powerful front-runner. For a lap I seemed to succeed.

"Suddenly, he sprinted by me, applied pressure, and I broke. Pre went on to win by two seconds, drawing me on to my fastest three-mile ever. Later, in what was at the time an uncharacteristic bit of openness on his part, he told me, 'I was hurting. If you'd gone hard for a couple of laps, you would have had me.'"

A Favorite of the Crowd

A month after the Pac-8 meet, Pre returned to Seattle for the NCAA meet. He easily won the three-mile, saving himself for the AAU the next weekend. "This has to rank way down the list of thrills for me," he said. "I needed a good workout, and that's about what I got."

The AAU Championships were in Eugene, and a packed house gave Pre a thunderous ovation when he stepped out onto the track. Pre smiled and waved to his people. After some light jogging, he went to the medical tent where trainer Larry Standifer was ready for what was by now pre-race ritual. "After a few minutes of rubdown, he would ask 'Am I tight?'" Standifer relates. "Of course, my answer would be, no, that he was really nice and loose. I would then ask him what he was going to run the race in. He would give me some mumbo jumbo and then go warm up. After the race got under way, sure enough, his lap times would settle down to whatever he had told me."

After a mile in 4:18.3, Pre took the lead and pushed hard, with Shorter, Len Hilton of the University of Houston, and Steve Stageberg of Georgetown behind. With two laps to go, Prefontaine threw in a 63.7 quarter-mile, which dropped everyone but the surprising Stageberg, who was reputed to have one of the best oxygen uptake rates ever tested. This Steve had grown up in Eugene but had left to attend Georgetown.

"We were both from Oregon, I from Eugene, he from Coos Bay, and yet he was the favorite of the Eugene crowd—I was the outsider," Stageberg muses.

Down the backstretch of the last lap, as hard as Pre pushed, Stageberg responded, until the last turn, when Pre finally began to pull away to win the three-mile by 10 yards in 12:58.6.

"Did I look tough?" Pre asked impishly afterward. Then he looked at the crowd and said, "Those people are fantastic. They're my people, man. How can you lose with 12,000 people behind you?"

As for Stageberg, he ran 13:00.4. Bowerman came up to him and "mentioned that Steve had a closer call than anyone had expected from me. My reply was, I should have won. I marveled at his outstanding accomplishments, but I never feared him."

Steve Prefontaine usually made an impression on those he met. For Blaine Newnham, the sports editor of the Eugene newspaper, *The Register-Guard*, from 1972–1982, the experience was a vivid one. The site: the 1971 U.S.-U.S.S.R. meet at Berkeley, California, a week after the AAU. Newnham was at the time working for a local paper and was assigned to interview the precocious Oregon star.

"He was standing on a balcony overlooking a swimming pool at the University of California," Newnham wrote. "I introduced myself.

"'I'm not talking to reporters anymore,' he said. 'I've decided that I'd better keep my mouth shut around newspaper people.' I mentioned his race against the Russians. I asked about his strategy and about pace. His eyes twinkled. He leaned back against the edge of the balcony and started talking about Harald Norpoth and Michel Jazy, two of the great European runners. 'I thought you weren't going to talk to sports writers anymore?' I asked.

"'You haven't asked me any stupid questions yet,' he said."

Pre set the first of his many American and collegiate records in that meet, though the race was somewhat atypical of his style. Bill Dellinger, the coach for the U.S. team, advised the two Steves—Prefontaine and Stageberg—to share the pacing chores to shake off the Russians. Pre had the odd numbered laps, Stageberg the even.

"We were on schedule," recalls Stageberg, "as I led at the mile in 4:17. I ran another 300 meters in the lead anxiously awaiting Steve's taking over, but he didn't and I finally looked back to see what was the problem. 'Keep the lead,' said Pre, 'I can't take it.' I realized the burden was all on me at the crucial point of the race, when we were all tired from the AAU meet the prior week. The Russians were still hanging on, and the weather was hot.

"As I recall, Steve finally helped out on the seventh or eighth lap and went on to win in an American 5000-meter record of 13:30.4."

From Berkeley, the AAU team, of which Pre was a member, went to Durham, North Carolina, for a match against a team from Africa. There, Prefontaine's threat came not from Stageberg, who began to lose form, but from Ethiopian Miruts Yifter, a future Olympic gold medalist.

In sweltering 87-degree heat, Pre led through the first two miles in slow times of 4:25.3 and 9:01.2. Yifter clung to him, until, with 700 yards to go, he started a furious, fabulous kick. Briefly, Steve went with him, then eased off from the sub-60 second pace. Yifter dashed up the home straight, got the gun for the last lap . . . and stopped. Apparently, he had thought the race was over. Pre stepped around him and continued on for a 13:57.6 5000-meter win.

Yifter was crushed. Yes, he had thought the race was over. Could he have beaten Pre over an extra lap? "Absolutely."

Pre was unpersuaded. "When he took off like that, I figured that either he had miscounted the laps or that he was just testing me to see how strong I was. I was prepared to come back at him on the last lap, though. It's really a tragedy—I feel sorry for him," Pre concluded.

Over Hills and in Arenas

Cross country was an enjoyable sport for Pre, one he liked in college as much as track, according to Bill Dellinger. He liked to get out on the varying terrain and show the longer distance men that he could be tough over six miles, too. After his freshman year, Steve never lost a cross country race, and in truth, was extended by the competition only in the bigger meets. One of those was at the NCAA Cross Country Championships at Knoxville, Tennessee, in the fall of 1971, his junior year. Pre had easily won the Pac-8 meet at UCLA, but Oregon as a team had taken second. The school was willing to send him but not the team. Pre would have none of it. He stated that he would not defend his NCAA title unless the entire team was sent.

It was, and it won.

At Knoxville, Pre again faced Garry Bjorklund, who had missed the previous NCAA cross country meet because of appendicitis.

"It was a beastly hilly course," says Bjorklund with relish. "We started up a big hill and came crashing down. We went through the mile in 4:24. There was still a group at three miles, so I took off and just started running as hard as I could. At four miles, I started to hurt pretty bad. Pre started to chip at me a little bit. At the top of a big hill, he sneaked away and got about 30 yards ahead. I closed and I closed, but couldn't catch him."

Steeplechaser Doug Brown of the University of Tennessee was also in the race and remembers the Prefontaine-Bjorklund struggle with some awe. "Near the end of the course it looped around, so you could see the guys ahead of you. The look on Pre's face—he was hurting so bad. He was like a strong bull, like a boxer on the cross country course. Pre just refused to accept the fact that somebody was going to be better than him in the United States."

A brief two month respite following cross country merged into the different world of indoor racing. In numbers, the races

Steve (bottom left) found his talent in high school when he lettered in cross country his freshman year.

Steve was a daily fixture on the streets of Coos Bay, typically running four to eight miles a day.

A common sight—Steve finishing first with no one in sight.

Despite chilly weather, Steve broke the national high school record in the two-mile by 6.9 seconds in April of his senior year.

A relaxed Pre won the state mile championship his senior year in 4:08.4, easily outdistancing Doug Crooks of North Eugene.

A few hours after winning the mile, Steve edged rival Mark Hiefield in the two-mile for his second title of the day at the state championships.

Marshfield High School 1969 yearbook. Only graduation could end Steve's two-year win streak in a state known for its excellent distance runners.

Pre got his first taste of international competition in a July 1969 meet against the Soviet Union in Los Angeles. He stayed with the front-runner for the first mile of the 5000 meters before fading to fifth.

Pre's last defeat in a cross country race came at the 1969 NCAAs. He was able to top John Bednarski of the University of Texas at El Paso and Donal Walsh of Villanova, but Gerry Lindgren of Washington State was too strong.

Steve's fierce competitiveness and all-out effort made him a favorite with the fans. Because of his relentless front-running, many of his opponents set personal records when they ran against him.

1969 University of Oregon cross country team. Head coach Bill Bowerman (wearing hat) and assistant coach Bill Dellinger (standing left) had their sights set on Pre (bottom middle) since his sophomore year in high school.

Two prodigies discuss race strategies before the 1969 NCAA Cross Country Championships in New York City. Gerry Lindgren (right) made the 1964 Olympic team just out of high school.

Pre's two-mile victory in a dual meet against UCLA in April 1970 came an hour after he tied for first in the mile at the same meet.

1970 Pac-8 Conference Championships, Los Angeles: Pre won the three-mile by 50 yards over Don Kardong of Stanford, Hartzell Alpizar of UCLA, Ole Oleson of USC, who finished second, and Herm Atkins of Washington.

After the 1970 Oregon Twilight meet, University of Oregon president Robert Clark and his wife, Opal, congratulate Pre for his sub-4:00-mile performance.

Pre set a meet record in his first NCAA three-mile championship in Des Moines, Iowa, in 1970. The first five finishers beat the old record, held by Gerry Lindgren of Washington State since 1966.

In a July 1970 U.S.—West Germany meet in Stuttgart, Harald Norpoth of West Germany trailed Pre for 4750 of the 5000 meters before unleashing a potent kick to take the victory. Trailing Norpoth is Kenny Moore, now a senior writer for Sports Illustrated.

1971 NCAA Championships, Seattle: Pre strode easily in front of Greg Fredericks of Penn State and Len Hilton of Houston as he set a meet record in capturing his second three-mile championship.

Avenging his previous year's fifth-place finish, Pre edged out Steve Stageberg of Georgetown by 10 yards, with Frank Shorter of the Florida Track Club trailing, for the 1971 AAU Championship victory in the three-mile at Hayward Field in Eugene, Oregon.

Steve Stageberg led for much of the race, but Pre raced to an American record in the 5000 meters at a 1971 U.S.–U.S.S.R. meet in Berkeley, California.

Sportscaster Jack Whitaker interviewed Pre after his record-setting 5000-meter performance in the 1971 U.S.–U.S.S.R. All-Star meet.

1971 NCAA Cross Country Championships, Knoxville, Tennessee: Garry Bjorklund of Minnesota tried to keep the lead, but Pre won his second cross country championship.

In June 1972, Pre attended a testimonial dinner for his retiring Marshfield High coach, Walt McClure.

In what many Oregon fans consider his best race ever, Pre takes the lead from teammate Rick Ritchie in the 1500-meter race against Oregon State's Hailu Ebba—the race Pre "should have lost."

1972 NCAA Championships, Eugene, Oregon: Once again, Pre beat Greg Fredericks of Penn State in the 5000 for his third consecutive championship.

Don Chadez

"So, it was in Eugene, Pre had won, the fans were going crazy as usual, and he came over to me and asked me to take a jog lap with him. He said it was a heckuva race, despite the fact that I'd lost. This was a different side of Pre from what I had known before."——Greg Fredericks

At a 1972 awards banquet to honor Oregon athletes, Pre is shown with fellow honorees Geoff Petrie, a guard for the NBA's Portland Trail Blazers, and high school javelin thrower Russ Francis.

were few during his career, but in excitement, the close confines of arenas packed with partisan crowds made them some of the most memorable of Steve Prefontaine's career.

At the beginning of 1972, the Olympic year, he raced in the *Los Angeles Times* Indoor meet hoping to meet George Young, the 34-year-old former world-record holder at two miles.

"Goldarn," Pre said when told that Young was bypassing the race. "I wanted to run against Young more than anybody in the field. I wanted to test the veteran out," he told *Sports Illustrated*. "I almost said the old man, but I don't want to make him mad and give him something to use against me when we race. Besides, he's not really old. And I like him a lot. He's super intelligent. And very good looking. And has a great family. And I hope he remembers all these nice things I'm saying when we do race."

Instead, Pre was up against Kerry O'Brien of Australia, the indoor two-mile world-record holder, and Emiel Puttemans, considered a threat at the coming Olympic Games. Pre ran away with the race in 8:26.6, with Puttemans a half-lap behind.

"He sure is a speedy little bug," O'Brien conceded. "I just wish I could have met that little bug last year."

"And I wish he'd stop calling me a little bug," Pre responded. "But wasn't that a super race?"

As Pre entered the outdoor season leading up to the Olympic Trials and Games, his confidence was at an all-time high. He had not lost a race at any distance over a mile in a year-and-a-half. He held American and collegiate records in the 5000 meters and had won the gold medal in the 1971 Pan Am Games in Cali, Colombia. His effect upon the fans at Hayward Field was by this time palpable.

Geoff Hollister, a former Oregon runner who had entered the Navy before Pre's arrival on campus, remembers the atmosphere upon his return to Eugene. "Warming up at Hayward Field felt different now. The minute Pre hit the field for his jog, there was an undercurrent of enthusiasm in the crowd. It surfaced in slight cheers as he raced down the stretch. You could feel the electricity."

Hollister was testing an experimental racing flat with a rubber sole developed by Bill Bowerman called the "Waffle." Someone suggested Pre try out a pair. "We both stood up," Hollister remembers, "and Pre looked me right in the eye. 'No, when you're gonna run the last lap in 57, you've gotta have spikes on your feet!'

"The more I thought about it, the more I liked what I had just heard. The guy told me exactly what was on his mind. It is part of track history now, but Pre went out and ran even 60s and finished with a 57 for just under 3:57 for the mile."

3

Spirit, Fierce and Driving

Of the thousands of people who knew Pre, each has their own sense of what he was "really" like. There was, of course, the public Pre, who by the spring of his junior year was no longer a precocious youngster out of Coos Bay, but a bona fide contender for a medal in the upcoming Olympic Games.

What attracted the legions of fans, however, was something more than a string of victories on the track. Ralph Mann would become Pre's friend and European traveling companion in the summers after Munich. He comments on the charisma that surrounded the well-publicized figure of Steve Prefontaine.

"He had this magnetism that just drew people toward him. He had the personality that people would just take to. It was strange, because many times we discussed it and he said it was just the way he acted, nothing unnatural. He didn't know what it was, and I couldn't figure it out just by watching it. . . ."

Everyone noticed it, including his competitors.

"I remember it was a cold day," rival and Oregon teammate Paul Geis says, of the first time he met Pre in June 1972. "The NCAA Championships were at Eugene, and everybody was in the trainer's tent trying to stay away from the wind and stay warm. He came in, and I remember distinctly that he had a sort of magnetism about him. I can't really explicitly say what it was—maybe it was because people said to him as he walked by, 'Go Pre,' or 'Go get 'em.' Maybe it was just his confidence, his sense of calmness."

Whatever that quality was, few were immune to it, either by a dismissal of Pre as "cocky" or by an ill-disguised adulation that extended to members of the Oregon team.

"It was hard for a lot of people to talk to him, because they held him in such awe," Scott Daggatt, who was to become one of his good friends, recalls. "When you have someone who is kind of a folk hero, you let him do all the talking. It took me a couple of years to get that out of me, to where I could say, 'Hey, look, I disagree with you.'"

A Whirlwind of Activity

The "public" wanted to know more about this outspoken Prefontaine. Ted Brock, writing for *Sport* magazine, visited with Pre in early 1972.

"The scenario for the film *GO PRE* begins at 6 A.M. on a Monday morning in early March. In a soiled sweatsuit and mud-lined shoes, Steve takes an early run of four or five miles ("quality running" at a six-minute-mile pace) along the roads of Eugene's Glenwood district and into Springfield. Having finished the day's first workout, he returns to his trailer home on a bank of the Willamette River to shower and uniform himself for the day: Levi jacket, jeans, an old pair of cross country shoes and one of his myriad printed T-shirts bearing the name of some recent track meet. He drives to sociology class in a light blue MGB convertible. This is the only piece of equipment that seems conspicuously out of place, though it's a cut below the Datsun 240-Z that it replaced—both cars no doubt holdovers from youthful Coos Bay dreams of cruisin' the main in a clean machine. Baby Blue, festooned with stickers showing ducks running hurdles and jumping through block O's, waits in a parking place outside the athletic office while Pre walks past, nodding and waving to undergraduates on his way to sociology.

"'I hate the image of being a super jock, an untouchable,' he remarks. 'When I'm on campus, I'll walk by a group of people and they'll whisper "Guess who just walked by." These are things I know I have to live with, but still they can get me down once in a while. That's one of the reasons I'm living in the trailer.'

"Sociology is over, and Pre stops off at the athletic office. As if on cue, his girlfriend Mary [Marckx] appears and the two exchange smiles and a brief greeting. The fairy tale tries to surface again, showing a picture of the wide-eyed 3.0 student-athlete with the pretty blonde beside the sports car. But reality reappears minutes later, following the drive home, in the form of a yellow slip of paper hanging from the screen door of the trailer. The gas bill has arrived. 'Ed's Propane. Mr. Prefontaine. $5.44.' No return address. The car is still running. Pre drives to the office marked 'River Bank Trailer Park,' gets out, and walks past the puddles and through the door with the Williams Bread-in-the-blue-gingham-wrapper decal. The manager knows Ed's address. Other side of town. Maybe there's time to pick up some food stamps along the way.

"It galls Prefontaine that he has to live the way he lives because of what he is—a long-distance runner. 'Amateurism is a thing that should have been kicked out in 1920, you know,' he says. 'The true amateurs, by the standards that were set up in the 1890s, were the elite, who were already well-established and set up in clubs and didn't need money to compete. The average athlete now is finding it damn hard to make it. I get $101 a month from the university. Room and board. And then there's going to school, buying books, and everything else. It's pretty hard to make it.'"

Few but Prefontaine could. He was possessed of enormous energy, however, and he managed to make ends meet. His was a level of activity that extended beyond the track and classroom, into every endeavor he undertook. Often, he was over at Roosevelt Junior High School, tutoring kids, telling them of his upbringing and the things they themselves could achieve in life.

Bill Bowerman, his coach at Oregon, says it this way: "The thing about Pre that set him apart from other athletes at Oregon were the many other things he got involved in. He'd go out and help kids and run with the old joggers and old women. He'd go up and get involved in the program at the State Penitentiary. That was just the kind of guy he was. He was . . . an achiever. Way beyond the ordinary. Anything

On Pre: Bob Kennedy

The current American-record holder in the 3000 and 5000 meters, Kennedy was asked to compare and contrast his approach to the sport to Pre's, both on and off the track.

The thing about Pre is that he ran as hard as he could every race, and if you were going to beat him, you were going to have to run harder than he did.

How do I say this in a noncocky way: I think that I'm probably the closest American distance runner—along with Todd Williams and Alberto Salazar in the way they race—to Steve Prefontaine since Steve, on the track. It seems like, after Steve, people got into a sit-and-kick type attitude and mentality, and now we're trying to get away from that again.

From what I've heard, Pre's personality and his running style were very similar: very confident in himself, brash, flamboyant—and that's how he ran. Just taking charge.

I'm very different from that. I'm relatively quiet, pensive, usually keep to myself in my thoughts and words, and try to go all out on the track. When we get on the track, Pre and I are very similar, but when we get off the track, we're a lot different.

I'm sure there are some parallels. I am a very competitive person in general, and that's what I love about running, the competition. I'm not too thrilled on the 15-mile runs. But I do it because I love to compete, and I know I have to do that in order to compete. It's the same way in other games. I'm not going to say that I always win, but nine times out of ten, I'll come out on top somehow, no matter what it is—anything!

Kennedy placed fifth in the 1996 Olympic 5000 meters, the highest finish by an American since Prefontaine's fourth place in 1972.

this guy went into, he was achieving about 200 percent. Tremendous energy."

An example of this energy, spontaneously repeated by different members of the Oregon team who knew Pre, is the "locker room" story.

"Pre was not easygoing in any way," says Paul Geis. "Everything had to be competitive or fast. You could come in from a workout, and have gotten out of your clothes and be already walking to the shower when Pre came in. And yet, by the time you came out of the shower, he would have gotten undressed, have already showered, dressed, and be shaking the water from his hair, anxious to get on the road. He was just always in a rush. It was a phenomenon."

In the spring of 1972, Pre began to look for a roommate to share the trailer he'd bought in Glenwood, a light industrial area interspersed with modest homes, situated between Eugene and Springfield. He wanted someone low-key, with whom he could get along. For the next year, through the Olympic Trials, the Games, and the post-Olympic 1973 season, Pat Tyson was that roommate. He provides a personal glimpse into the offtrack world of the Steve Prefontaine of that time.

"When Steve asked if I wanted to room with him, the first thing I thought was that it was going to be cheap—like $30 a month. I'm a tightwad, so I jumped at it. Here was someone I could train with in the morning, who has good hours, and so on. I knew that sometimes living with someone that well-known can be tough on you, but I thought, 'Well, this could be interesting.'

"It was a small place—not much privacy. But he was very kind, considerate. I lived there a year-and-a-half, and we never had a fight, never argued. The phone would ring a lot. I almost felt that I was Prefontaine's Answering Service, but I didn't really feel that way.

"I began to settle down a little bit for the first time, seeing him so hyperactive. I thought my day was filled up, and I saw him doubling that. He'd often do two things at once. Instead of just writing a letter, he'd be writing a letter and eating at the same time.

"His diet was pretty good really, considering. It seemed like he was dieting a lot—he had to do that to stay at his 145 pounds because he'd go up over 150 pretty easily. If I fixed anything, he'd eat it. For breakfast, we had pancakes or french toast or something like that. For dinner, we'd make a lot of salads—Pre liked fresh, green, tossed salads. He'd buy meat and would usually end up saying, 'You can have the meat, and I'll just have salad.' He would think he was eating good, but there were a lot of times when he would go out and get junk food or go over to the Paddock Tavern.

"After a meet, we might go out for dinner and have a couple of beers. Steve wasn't one to sit back and think. He'd go from table to table and visit. He liked to move about and talk to people.

"Pre was what you would call a 'toucher'. He wasn't scared to come up and look you in the eye and touch you. He was a very warm person. He'd hug you, and in this society the way it is, you don't hug other males. But Pre was never ashamed to do that, ever.

"He liked to swim in the summer. We'd go pool-hopping at the various motels. Lay in the sun. We liked to sit back in his convertible—Mary, myself, and Pre— take off someplace down the coast, to Coos Bay or someplace, and Mary and I would sing old songs from the 1950s and 1960s. Pretty soon Pre would get into that, too, and we'd get our own little natural high. . . ."

"A Race Pre Should Have Lost"

He did not suffer adversity gladly. Pre's 1972 track campaign started with a two-mile race in a dual meet against Fresno State, held in Fresno. The wind was terrible, swirling to gusts of 30 mph, and Pre's plans for a good time went awry. He finished in 8:55.4, and his pique, according to one eyewitness, was something to behold.

"He started cursing afterward, and swearing that he would never go near that town again, and it was just the worst dump he'd ever run in, as if to say what the hell are the citizens trying to do, bringing the weather in on him when he was going to treat them to a bravura performance. . . ."

It is likely that Steve felt more kindly toward the citizens of Bakersfield when, a week later, he started his Olympic buildup in earnest there with a 27:22.4 collegiate six-mile record.

"They'll hear about this in Europe," Pre crowed. "They have to be respecting me more now and wondering if I have any weaknesses."

Pre and Oregon assistant coach Bill Dellinger worked on those weaknesses. The training during that spring put Pre in the best shape of his life, and those who knocked Pre's supposed lack of a finishing kick were somewhat subdued by a race many longtime Oregon fans think was his best ever.

It came the week after the Washington State dual meet, in which Pre set an American 5000-meter record in 13:29.6. His fans were still buzzing about that one as they filled the stands at Hayward Field for the meet against Oregon State. The team race was predicted to be a close one, and instrumental for the respective teams were Prefontaine for Oregon and Hailu Ebba for Oregon State. It was unclear exactly which events the two would be competing in. Pre in the 1500 and Ebba in the 800 perhaps.

But at the line for the start of the 1500 were both Pre and Hailu. The anticipation was intense as the fans got to their feet for the gun.

Here was Pre, the immovable object, against the faster Ebba, the irresistible force. Oregon's Rick Ritchie led through the first lap before Pre took off, with Ebba close behind. Through the next two laps, the graceful Ethiopian tracked him, and Pre continued to pour on the pace. "That was a great race," recalls a teammate, "because it was a race Pre should have lost."

On the backstretch, Ebba tried to go by, and Prefontaine dug deeper. The stands were in turmoil, as Pre's people hysterically urged him on. Around the last bend, Ebba made another bid, and Pre took him out into lane three to keep him from going by. Up the homestretch Ebba broke, and Pre had the race in a personal record 3:39.8. It was a great race, the quintessential Prefontaine race.

Still the Best

The goal of beating Prefontaine was a high one, not one that most contemporaries could undertake with a realistic chance of success, given Pre's consistency and mental toughness. One runner who had the tools was Penn State's Greg Fredericks, and he felt a special motivation to beat Prefontaine, preferably in Eugene.

"I'd kinda gotten a bad taste in the NCAA the year before, when it was at Washington," he says. "I knew at the time that I had a fatigue fracture and hadn't been training well. [Fredericks took second.] Anyway, Pre's whole thing after that meet was, well, there really wasn't anybody in the race; he had trained hard all week, and he had gone out and jogged through it.

"So I was really gung-ho the whole next year, 1972, trying to get into good enough shape to say, 'I'm going to stick with the guy and possibly beat him in the end.'"

All races were in meters at the 1972 NCAA Championshiops because of the Olympic year. As a result, the three-mile was changed to the 5000 meters. The race was fast from the start as Pre took the lead after the half-mile and clicked off 4:21.8 and 4:25.6 mile splits. He and Fredericks were 30 yards ahead of the field and pulling away. Pre pushed and came up with a third mile in 4:16.9, which finally opened a 15-yard gap on Fredericks.

"The difference at the end was just a couple of seconds worth," Fredericks muses. "I think I had a mental lapse with a half-mile to go. He got out on me and you get to a point where you notice, all of a sudden, that he's gotten away, and you have a complete letdown."

Pre broke the tape in 13:31.4 for his third consecutive NCAA title in the same event. With the end of the college track season, Pre could now focus entirely on winning an Olympic medal.

4

The Olympics

"At some time on Thursday, July 6, it began to take shape as America's greatest distance race of all time." So wrote Cordner Nelson, co-founder of *Track & Field News*, of the feeling that pervaded Eugene before the finals of the 5000 meters in the 1972 U. S. Olympic Trials. The race had all of the elements: Pre in front of his home crowd; George Young, former world-record holder in the two-mile, opting to test Pre for the first time; and the presence of some fine distance men, including Tracy Smith, Gerry Lindgren, and Greg Fredericks.

The match between the 34-year-old Young and the 21-year-old Prefontaine caused much excitement in particular.

"There was some sort of an effort on the part of the media to build up a 'grudge' race between the two of us," Young recalls. "It never developed because of the mutual respect we had for each other."

Nevertheless, there was the feeling that if Pre was going to suffer his first defeat at his distance in Eugene, George Young would be the man to do it—he had experience, speed, and extraordinary toughness. Pre-like toughness.

On Sunday, July 9, 12 men toed the line for the start. The weather was warm but not stifling. Gerry Lindgren led past the 880-yard mark in 2:09.6, before drifting back through the pack. Pre took over and averaged around 66 seconds for a quarter-mile lap through 1½ miles. Then Pre ran laps of 64.7 and 65.1, stringing out the pack. Only Young moved with him quickly and was close with 3½ laps to go. Nelson calls the race:

"Now Pre began the task of breaking Young, one of the gutsiest runners in track history. Pre ran a lap in 63.4, which dropped Hilton 25 yards behind, but the veteran Young held on grimly. With the crowd roaring, Prefontaine began a remarkable drive. A lap in 61.5 weakened Young and left Hilton 75 yards back, but Pre was only beginning. He increased the pace and opened an eight-yard lead with a lap to go. Young had to surrender, and Pre completed the lap in 58.7. With Young beaten, Pre slowed in the homestretch. Then he thought better of it and picked up for a respectable finish in 13:22.8, a time bettered only by Clarke (twice) and Dave Bedford's 13:22.2."

Marty Liquori was there at the finish. "The thing I remember about it was that coming off the last turn, Pre was completely dead—just wobbling up the straightaway. He hit the inside rail and almost stumbled, and the fans were loving it, because he was completely spent when he hit the line."

For Bill Dellinger, the memory is of the crowd when Pre made his break from Young. "I remember standing in the middle of the field and yelling at Pre as loud as I could and not being able to hear my own voice. It had become a deafening noise so that you couldn't even hear yourself."

Later, as Pre signed autographs for the multitudes, he explained to Blaine Newnham what it meant to run in front of his people.

"I'll tell you one thing, I love every one of them. I've thought about the Olympic Games every day of my life since 1968, but there is a breaking point in each race when you wonder if all the sacrifice is really worth it. You think 'why should I do this? I don't have to run this hard.' But that's when I think about them. They keep me going."

Then in a typical gesture, Pre asked his beaten opponent, George Young, to jog a victory lap with him. Later, as he signed autographs, Pre was asked how it felt to be number one? "Well, all I can say is I hope I can stay fit, and if I'm able to run like this in Munich, I'm going to be pretty hard to stop."

Pre suggested that Young stay in Eugene for a few weeks and "burn up the mountains" with him. With regret, Young had to decline.

Final Preparations

With the Trials behind him—and a success—Pre continued his severe training. As always, Dellinger handled the workouts, while Bowerman acted as counselor and sounding board in the once-a-week bull sessions at the coach's house up on the butte overlooking the McKenzie River.

More than anything Pre wanted to be prepared for a race that would test everyone in the field to their maximum.

"I could lose and live with the knowledge that I'd given 120 percent, given it all, if I'd been beaten by a guy who came up with 130 percent," Pre said in early 1972. "But to lose because I'd let it go to the last lap . . . I'd always wonder whether I might have broken away. . . ."

Dellinger, himself a medal winner in the 1964 Olympic 5000, knew what was needed and fed it to Pre. One workout was four 1320s and 3 × 1-mile with the times decreasing on each repetition. In his own Olympic preparation eight years before, Dellinger had done the 1320s in 3:15, 3:13, 3:11, and 3:09. The workout became a challenge to Pre, and it didn't take him long to "gobble it up," in Dellinger's apt phrase. Before Munich, Pre ran 3:12, 3:09, 3:06, and 3:00, then came back with the cut-down miles.

For sharpening, Dellinger had him run a solo mile under 4:00. Just walk to the line, get set, then click off a mile in 3:59, with no competition and no psyche except the impetus of the Olympic 5000-meter, when 21-year-old Steve would be going against the "veterans."

He was very aware of his relative youth and of the trend he was trying to buck. "There are big odds against me," he conceded. "Nobody under 25 has ever won the Olympic five. But if everything goes right, whoever wins will know he has been in one helluva race."

In order to sharpen the Olympic athletes' training, the United States Olympic Committee set up a mandatory training camp in July. At the training camp in Maine, Pre continued to prepare. "If anything, I may be putting in too much mileage," he allowed.

He left for Oslo, Norway, and a series of tune-up meets for the Games. One was a 1500-meter, in which Pre ran a fine 3:39.4, getting second to eventual 1500-meter Olympic champion Pekka Vasala's 3:38.3.

"I didn't mind getting second," he wrote to a friend. "He's the best in the world."

The second day of the two-day meet, Pre came back with an American 3000-meter record of 7:44.2, demolishing Jim Beatty's mark by 10 seconds. "I could have broken the world record if I hadn't run the 1500 the night before," Steve said.

His running was going well, but the pressure was definitely being felt. "I can hardly wait to get back," Pre wrote to Pat Tyson on one of the dozens of postcards he sent weekly to all and sundry. "I can't wait for this damn running to be over with. Pre." And again on August 1, the day before the 1500-meter in Oslo: "I'll sure be glad when all of this is over with."

To add to the tension, he hurt his foot slightly while training and had to watch from the sidelines two weeks after his 3000-meter race as Lasse Viren of Finland went past 3000 meters in 7:43.6 on his way to an 8:14.0 two-mile world record. Pre felt frustrated, saying that he would have broken that world record, too, if he had been able to run in the race.

The Viren mark provided incentive. His foot better, Pre set an American record of 8:19.4 in a two-mile race in Munich just before the Opening Ceremonies. It was a dark, windy evening at the Post track on the outskirts of Munich. The race was actually a 3000-meter, but Bowerman and Dellinger measured out the extra distance and when Pre passed the finish line of the 3000 he just kept going, dodging perplexed officials, who wondered, no doubt, what this crazy American runner was up to.

Going for the Gold

Pre looked ready. Now came the waiting period before the heats of the 5000-meter, the days spent wandering around Munich or the Olympic Village, trying to keep the tension bearable and the homesickness under control.

On Pre: Alberto Salazar

As other kids who were aspiring baseball players might hear of Babe Ruth, that's how I would hear about Pre. His front-running example reinforced in my mind that that was the way you showed what you were made of—lead from the front, not just wait in the back.

He wouldn't take second effort—it wasn't acceptable. It was all out. When you're like that, when you start doing that, you become a lot more consistent. And that's what you saw with Pre. The guy never had races out the back end. I think it comes down to pride in the end. Not proud, necessarily, that you're better than everybody else, but that you are tougher than anybody else. That if you lose, you are going to make whomever you are running against pay. And that's what Pre did.

At a very young age, he was competitive with the best in the world. He certainly wasn't scared of running against whomever. Like at the Olympics, you see the kind of person he was. You look at the way he ran it, he really went for it and tried to win the whole darn thing. There's no doubt in my mind he could have gotten third if he had sat back and timed his kick just right. But he didn't want third place. He wanted to give it everything to see if he could win the gold.

I think in 1976 in Montreal, he would have given Viren a fight like hell. I mean, it would have been unbelievable.

Alberto Salazar is the former American-record holder in the 5000 and 10,000 meters and marathon.

Dan Berger was covering for the Associated Press at the time:

"I was having a cup of coffee in the press room set up by Adidas in the Olympic Village when Pre walked in and sat down a few seats away. He looked tired. He smiled and returned my hello, said he felt fine, and so forth. Nothing major.

"I was about to slide over and interview him when a European journalist plopped down into the seat I had planned to use and introduced himself to Steve. He began to ask a series of questions all relating to the running tactics which would be used in the 5000 final. Pre knew he would be in for a tough race, he said. (And I began to realize that his comments were being said softly, not brashly as I had imagined he would act.) He talked of what kind of a pace he felt it would be. He said he felt he'd have to push the pace midway in the race, because if it turned into a kicker's race, he'd be in trouble. He said he had a lot of respect for Viren and the others.

"I didn't take any notes, but I was impressed with the way Steve handled the interview like a professional. Not arrogant. Not bragging. Just matter-of-factly setting down his feelings."

Pre's plans for the race were shattered by the terrorist attack upon Israeli athletes within the Olympic Village by elements of what was then termed an Arab terrorist group. Several Israelis died in the initial assault. The remaining hostages were killed a day later during a bungled rescue attempt by the West German authorities. A total of 12 athletes and coaches lost their lives.

Knowing Steve would be upset, Dellinger went to the Village, vaulted a fence, and brought him out. They went to Austria, an hour away, and spent the day up in the mountains. Pre took a run and tried to forget. When they returned to Munich, Bill had him move into his apartment rather than return to the Village.

Though still shaken, Pre looked good in the qualifying heats, running a fast 13:32.6 behind Emiel Puttemans of Belgium. But beneath his surface calm, he was extremely upset, first by the tragedy itself, which stole all of the glamour of the Games for him, and also by the change in the time schedule caused by the memorial service for the slain athletes.

"Pre felt that the extra day of rest was going to be really advantageous to those who had run the 10,000," Dellinger explains. "Which it was, of course. I tried to counsel him that you can't let these type of things bother you."

The day of the final was muggy, with the sun heating the track beneath the transluscent canopy that covered one-third of the stadium. An expectant sell-out crowd of over 80,000 waited for the start. A group of spectators who could not get tickets clustered on the berm created from World War II rubble 300 yards from the stadium. The 13 finalists approached the line, perhaps the strongest field of 5000-meter runners in Olympic history: Lasse Viren, who had set a world record in winning the 10,000-meter gold earlier in the Games, and Juha Vaatainen of Finland; Dave Bedford and Ian Stewart of Great Britain; Mohamed Gamoudi of Tunisia; Pre's old nemesis, Harald Norpoth of West Germany. And Steve Prefontaine.

Then, after all the anticipation, the pace for the final was painfully slow, even slower than the first 5000 of the 10,000-meter race. They passed two miles at a trot, in 8:56.4. This was not the race Pre had said he would run. He had wanted a race where it came down to "who's toughest," and this was a kicker's race. But there was no way Pre was going to let that continue.

With four laps to go, he chopped the 67-second pace with a lap in 62.5, then one in 61.2. He dropped many in the 13-man field with the 2:03.7 over two laps, but Lasse Viren was still there, as was Gamoudi, and Puttemans. Viren, in fact, put himself slightly in the lead, keeping the initiative, showing great poise for one who, at 23, was the youngest man in the field next to Pre.

The third lap of the buildup ended in 60.3, and at the bell, it looked like a three-man race among Pre, Gamoudi, and Viren, with Ian Stewart of Great Britain too far back for gold.

Viren still led slightly, with Pre behind him and Gamoudi off Pre's right shoulder. At the top of the backstretch, with 300 meters left, Pre started to pull out to pass Viren, but Gamoudi, one of those cagey vets Pre was so aware of, moved instantly to cut him off before he could get past Viren.

Chastened, Pre dropped behind Viren again until the top of the last curve, when he tried to go again. And again,

Gamoudi moved at the perfect moment to cut him off.

His momentum gone, Pre gathered one more time for the final straight, but when he tried to call up strength from deep within himself, there was no response. Totally spent, he staggered the last dozen meters and was passed by Stewart, running for a bronze medal. Viren won the gold in 13:26.4, with Gamoudi taking the silver.

The defeat was devastating. Pre sought solitude in the bowels of the Olympic Stadium, where Blaine Newnham of *The Register-Guard* from Eugene found him. Years later, the sportswriter recalls the scene:

"I said it was a nice race, I know you feel bad, but we've got to talk.

"He said, 'I've got nothing to say,' and he started off. All of a sudden, it was like there was an explosion in my head, and I said, 'Wait a minute, you've got to talk to me. What about all those people back in Eugene, the people at Hayward Field, Pre's People? They've lived this race with you, they can understand what happened, and we've got to talk.'

"I said, 'How old are you?' He said 21 or 22, I don't really remember what he was [21]. 'And so you finished fourth in the world, how bad is that?'

"He said, 'Well, that's not too bad.'

"I said, 'Did you run for third or second? No, you ran to win, you took the lead with a mile to go, you ran your butt off, and you finished fourth, now how bad is that?'

"'No, it wasn't that bad.'

"What he needed was someone to put his arm around him, to kind of hug him and say, it's okay, we understand. Pre's People understand. And so, goodness, he started up talking and 20 minutes later he was all pumped up again. And I remember Great Britain's David Bedford walking by, and he shouted at Bedford, 'I'll see you in Montreal and I'll kick your butt!'"

It was a strong trait in Pre. He didn't like to lose—hated it—and if he did, his first reaction was to make an excuse.

"The pace wasn't fast enough," he told Bert Nelson of *Track & Field News*. "If it had been 8:40 for the first two miles, I would have had gold or silver. It would have put crap in their legs. It was set up for Gamoudi and Viren." Infuriated that Gamoudi had cut him off not once, but twice, Pre vowed, "From now on, I'm going to be a dirty son of a bitch. I'm going to foul a lot of people. I'll probably get thrown out of a few races, but it's time we Americans learned to run like the Europeans."

Disillusioned as he was by his Munich experience, Pre could still see the lessons beyond his anger. "He didn't lose too many," Bowerman states, "but when he would, hell, he'd bounce back. He was just so fiercely competitive; and he could evaluate them. He'd go out there and run the best race he could and then, if he got whipped, why, there was another day; he learned from it. I don't think he ever thought he knew it all, anytime.

"He recognized that he was a kid running among men and the longer-distance races are men's races. I don't know of any distance performer who is not better at 25 than he was when aged between 18 and 22. He recognized his time was ahead of him."

A disheartened Pre was encouraged by the support he received when he returned to the States after two post-Olympic meets in Rome and London. "If anything will keep me running," he said, "it's the fantastic response. Complete strangers write wishing me well. The local people are so great. I would have to move away from Oregon. I couldn't retire here."

And even outside of Eugene, there was little gloating. Bob Payne of the Spokane *Spokesman-Review* in Washington described the sentiment most succinctly several years afterward.

"He didn't bring home a medal, but he helped create in that 5000 final one of the greatest, most wildly exciting distance races in history—forcing it through that incredible, four-minute, final mile, taking the lead with two laps to go, perhaps knowing already that he didn't have the late speed or the experience to hold all of 'em off. Viren, then Gamoudi, then Stewart, all got him, faster perhaps, wiser surely at the time. But none any gutsier.

"There was no grim satisfaction that the cocky little braggart had gotten his. He'd made the race, put himself on the line, never flagged. Given it everything. He always did."

5

Years of Thrilling Madness

Quickly, Steve settled back into the routine of the college student: attended classes, did his workouts, watched *Love, American Style* on TV, forgot to vote. Still, Pre returned from Munich a changed man.

Despite the support and good wishes of his community, he felt a depression resulting from his Olympic experience that was not to leave him fully for the next year-and-a-half. The disappointment was beyond ready assimilation.

True to a promise he had made to himself before Munich, Steve skipped the 1972 cross country season. He continued to live with Pat Tyson in the trailer, along with Lobo, a perhaps German Shepherd pup that Pre rescued on its way to the pound.

"All the next year, he taught Lobo and made him into a very disciplined dog," Tyson says. "Lobo was really his buddy."

Gradually, as the Oregon winter rains closed in on Pre and Lobo, doing workouts around the streets of Eugene and Springfield, the pain eased.

The Unbeatable Senior

The indoor track season of 1973 opened with Pre continuing his winning ways, although some competitors noticed that Steve now showed the ability to relate to them before he beat them into the track as well as after. "The defeat in Munich seemed to have sharpened his human side," Don Kardong observes, "to emphasize the qualities of warmth that he had hidden behind a veil of invincibility."

At the *Los Angeles Times* Indoor meet, he took on the milers at their own distance and beat them. "I didn't feel great with a half-mile to go," Pre said after his upset win in 3:59.2. "Then I heard the crowd come to life and I thought, 'Hell, they're right on my butt ready to pass me,' so I just dug down and ran as fast as I could."

Steve ran the last quarter-mile on the 160-yard track in 57.6, and beat, among others, Marty Liquori, a renowned miler who would one day hold the American record for 5000 meters. "I seem to be getting more speed the older I get," Pre enthused, outwardly as upbeat as ever.

In that race, as in many others, Prefontaine appeared to derive a direct energy from the crowds he performed before. It was a phenomenon that Liquori thinks might ultimately have hurt Pre by the time the important European races rolled around.

"Because so many times he would come to these indoor races and just kill the fields and win by a half a lap or so. I think the biggest thing in Pre's mind was to please the fans. He would respond to the crowd and pick up the pace before it should have been picked up, doing things that take a lot of mental and physical energy. I think it took a lot out of him. . . ."

That night, Pre went out and partied. Liquori was rooming with him at the meet hotel and remembers Steve coming back around 5:00 A.M.

"He woke me up to ask when I had to get up to catch my plane back East. At about 7:00, I got up and he got up with me and said, 'I'll help you carry your bags downstairs.' Then he went out on a 10-mile run."

Shortly after that indoor race, Pre spoke of the added incentive provided by the most special crowd, the one made up of the people of Eugene.

"This is my last year at Oregon," he said, "and it means a lot to me. The people have been great to me there, so if I have to run three races to win the Pac-8 team title, I'll do it. Oh, sure, I'll probably be tired, but the people shouting will carry me across the finish line."

He now began to work on regaining a measure of his Munich fitness. In a low-key all-comers meet in Bakersfield, California, in late March 1973, he ran his first competitive six-mile of the year and set an American record of 27:09.4. It was a harbinger of the great final collegiate season that he was to have.

The 85 to 90 miles of training per week that Pre had started in November continued until a week before a four-way meet with UCLA, Washington State, and Nebraska at Eugene in mid-April. "The week of the meet was the first time I rested in over four months," Pre said later in explaining a remarkable double victory.

With teammates Mark Feig and Scott Daggatt pulling him through a 59.1 first quarter in the mile race, Pre then took charge and ran to victory with laps of 59.9, 59.4, and 58.4.

"It was very easy," Pre declared of his 3:56.8. "I wasn't even pointing for that but just running the way I felt." An hour later, he returned for the three-mile and shook off his tiredness to record a 13:06.4 win over stubborn John Ngeno of Washington State. It was, at the time, the best one-day double ever, better even than Kip Keino's 3:53.1/13:31.6 races of 1967.

Pre now readied himself for the Oregon Twilight meet, an invitational meet for Oregon athletes that served as a prep race for the NCAA Championships. Despite his fabulous performance in the quadrangular meet, Steve was far from satisfied with his fitness. On the day of the Twilight meet mile, he twice told Coach Bill Dellinger that he didn't want to run because his legs were dead. Dellinger pointed to the 6,500 people in the stands and said, "Look at all those people; they came to see you run." Pre responded with a 3:55.0. At the time, only two Americans had ever run faster.

"Before any race, Pre would always say how he didn't feel good and didn't want to run," teammate Steve Bence recollects. "No matter where the race was or how important it was, he was saying, 'Aw, I wish I wasn't running; I don't think I'm going to run well. . . .' Then he'd go out and run like heck."

The self-doubt that plagues most runners—even Steve

Prefontaines—quickly disappeared after the challenge had been met and conquered. "I needed that," grinned Pre after his 3:55.0. "I think if I concentrated on the distance, I could be a pretty good miler. Bill told me I could have run 3:52 under better conditions. I think the world record [3:51.1 at the time] is in reach."

The spring of 1973 was Pre's final year of collegiate track. He had the enviable record of never having lost in a distance race over a mile at his home track. There were some close races and some where Pre almost played with his opponents. During the Pac-8 meet at Eugene that year, he was plagued by sciatica, a painful inflammation of the nerves in the back and in the back of the legs, yet defeated rival Ngeno on tactics as well as on foot racing. "I pulled every trick out of the hat, including making noises so he would think I was hurting more than I really was," Pre chuckled after that race.

The Search for an Heir-Apparent

Laughter was not forthcoming on another matter, however. As Pre was graduating that spring, the press had started looking for a worthy successor. Paul Geis seemed the likely candidate.

Geis had transferred from Rice University, in his home state of Texas, to the University of Oregon after experiencing the running atmosphere in Eugene the year before at the 1972 NCAA Championships. Training with the team and competing for the Oregon Track Club while he sat out his year of ineligibility, Geis began to run very well indeed. Bence, a friend of them both, explains:

"When Geis first came to Oregon, there was no problem. Paul was a good runner, but no threat to Pre. Perhaps there was some friction as they worked out together.

"Geis improved rapidly, and there was some resulting competition during practice, which Bill Dellinger discouraged. The press should be blamed for the true rivalry. They called Geis the 'heir-apparent' and made many comparisons. This put pressure an Geis to try and run as well as or better than Pre, and Pre must not have liked the idea that there was someone who could step in and fill his shoes. The result was two great Oregon distance runners competing against each other, not with each other."

The rivalry surfaced full-blown after the Pac-8 Conference meet. Ten days after beating Ngeno in the three-mile, Pre was running a two-mile in the Oregon Twilight II, his last race as a collegian in front of the home fans. A kind of farewell appearance.

Geis returned two days before the meet from California, where he had had his "drawers blown off" in the Vons Classic. He didn't want to compete in Eugene, but Dellinger told him to run for fun. Geis stuck with Pre the entire way until the last 220 yards and finished only 0.2 second behind Pre's excellent 8:24.6.

"It was the best race of my life at the time," Geis reflects. "There was no pressure, and I just stayed with him until a 220 to go. Afterward, he was really upset with me, just really mad, even though he'd destroyed me in the last 220. He had thought that I was going to share the pace with him, and that caused a lot of problems between us, because I was really hurt. It was my best time, and here was a guy that I wanted to be my friend, and I didn't know if I'd done the right thing or what. . . ."

Pre grumbled: "It was apparent I was doing all the work."

It was a rivalry that lasted to the end, one in which two proud people had the natural differences between them enlarged by the magnifying glass of the press. It reached its most comical point the next year in a two-mile race at a Hilites meet, similar to the Twilight meet, in Corvallis, Oregon. Dellinger insisted the two work together and not compete at the finish. "Pre and Geis finished hand-in-hand and staring at each other," Bence laughs. "Not in friendship but in distrust that the other would make a last-second lunge for the tape."

A Bid for a Fourth Title

Pre ran his last track race as an Oregon undergraduate in the 1973 NCAA Championships in the heat and humidity of Baton Rouge, Louisiana. He wasn't thrilled with the idea of sweating himself dry, but he was eager to win his fourth consecutive outdoor title in the same event, a feat never before accomplished.

It was a good field, with runners like Irishman John Hartnett of Villanova and Kenyan John Ngeno of Washington State entering the three- instead of the six-mile just to get a shot at Pre.

In the prelims, Steve ran harder than he had to and lowered the meet record to 13:19.0. That was the day Nick Rose of Great Britain, running for Western Kentucky, first met him.

"It was a really hot day, and I can remember I was sitting in the shade of the medical tent and Pre came up and started talking, which really freaked me out because I always sort of hero-worshiped him and looked up to him as a great runner. You sort of put these guys up on a pedestal and think they'll never talk to you. But he really surprised me."

The rest day before the finals on June 9 brought a typical whirl of activity. Pre had taken up photography, and as with all things he did, it was no halfhearted enterprise. In a borrowed car, he and Mark Feig drove through the Louisiana countryside, periodically stopping to snap pictures. For three hours, Pre took photos he would later develop in the dark room he had built back in Eugene. The trip outside of Baton Rouge also helped Pre get his mind off the final, for despite easily winning the prelims, he was worried.

His sciatica was perhaps the only serious running-related injury he ever suffered. When it did flare up, Pre was in big trouble.

"He was really afraid he was going to lose, because he hadn't done much training," Feig relates. "Yet he went out and forced the pace again in that race and ended up breaking the field. He was so tough."

After an 8:50.2 two-mile, Prefontaine crossed the finish line in 13:05.3 for a five-second victory over Ted Castaneda from the University of Colorado. "It was a matter of trying to catch a locomotive," Ted recalls.

Pre was equally impressed. "It's great to go out like this, to know that I've done something that nobody else has ever done gives me a warm feeling. Now I intend to spend the summer in Europe and show I'm better than the fourth-fastest in the world."

Steve Prefontaine had two distinctly different effects on his competitors. Some he intimidated into running worse than they otherwise might have; to others he posed a challenge they worked hard to match. At the AAU Championships the week after Baton Rouge, one runner made that leap of faith in his own ability and pushed Pre to a new U.S. three-mile record.

Dick Buerkle was three years out of Villanova University. He was talented and tough, but not thought to be in Pre's class. Through miles of 4:23.1 and 4:21.0, Buerkle dogged his opponent's tracks. Only in the last half-mile was Pre able to crack him.

"I was ready then," Buerkle states quietly. "I was really pushing from the mile on, running just about as hard as I could. When he took off with a half-mile to go, I just knew I couldn't hang in there any longer."

Pre won in 12:53.4, better than his American-record 5000 pace of the year before in the Olympic Trials. Buerkle broke 13 minutes by two-tenths.

"I didn't even think about running that fast," Buerkle admits. "I just said, 'I'm going to stay with this guy; I'm going to try and kick his butt.' I was out to knock him off then.

"I don't think that I was ever really afraid of Pre. I think I always felt that I could beat him. He was just one of those cocky kind of guys, dynamic kind of guys that you try to shoot at. He would stand up there and say 'come on and get me,' a king of the hill. I always wanted to get him. I didn't know when it was going to happen, but I knew I was going to keep working until I beat him. When I got that close at Bakersfield, I knew I just had to work a little harder and learn a little more. I felt that I was ready for him."

Buerkle would have to wait. Since the fall of 1969, no American had beaten Pre at any distance over a mile indoors or out. And none of the mile losses were runaways.

Sometimes Pre invited people to test his mortality. One such race was the Hayward Restoration meet on the weekend following the AAU.

On Pre: Mary Slaney

The first time I met Steve was in Europe in 1973. He was a member of the senior [U.S.] team, and it was my first international trip. Everybody was friendly to me, I was like the little sister to all these "older" people—they weren't really old, but you know.

As the six weeks of the tour progressed, I did all these workouts and these races, and I did okay, winning all of the races but one. Pre felt I was very talented, but that because of all the workouts I was doing and all the racing, and the pressure on someone that young (I turned 15 on the trip), I think he was just very concerned about "burnout"—that was the term he used.

We got back in late August, and in September, he started calling me, just to check up on me. I don't know why he took such an interest, I really don't. We became friends. He would call once a week, and the first Nike shoes I ever got were from Pre. He sent me a box of all these prototype shoes.

He was trying to get my mother to move the family to Eugene [from Southern California], and he talked to me and my mom about having Bill Bowerman

The University of Oregon was rebuilding the West grandstands at Hayward Field, and one method the athletic department used to raise money was by holding invitationals with Pre as the main attraction. He was selfless in offering his presence to help the fundraising and energetic in attracting top talent to run against him and to draw the Pre-hungry fans. For this race, he invited Dave Wottle, the Olympic 800-meter champion of the year before, to race at one mile.

"He said, 'why don't you come up to Eugene before we go over to Scandinavia, and we'll run a mile together and we'll try for the world record,'" Wottle recalls. "He said, 'I'll lead

coach me. It came to the point where he said that if Bowerman doesn't coach you , or you don't want Bowerman to coach you, then I would like to coach you. The family didn't move; that whole year wasn't a good year. He still called every week, and I wrote letters to him.

You never know what path he would have taken. He was such a dynamic personality. You don't know where he would have plugged himself into the sport right now, and how different our sport would be if he were still here. He had a way of getting people to take notice—not necessarily listen—but to take notice.

I think I was fortunate to have gotten to know him that well in that short of a time. For the life of me, I don't know why he took such an interest in me. And I don't really know why I came here to Eugene, and why this place means so much, why Hayward Field is the way it is, because it is definitely different than any other place.

I just wish that I had more time to know him than I did.

Mary Slaney is the only distance runner in history, male or female, to hold more American records than Steve Prefontaine.

you on the way, and you'll get a great time.'"

With just five days' notice, a crowd of 12,000 showed up to watch. Pre took over after the half and led through the 1320 in 2:56.0, with Wottle on his shoulder. With a little more than 220 to go, Wottle drove past and opened a 10-yard lead, which he held to the tape. Pre, who afterward complained that he had wanted to explode on the last lap but couldn't for some reason, nevertheless ran a lifetime best of 3:54.6, second to Wottle's 3:53.3.

Bill Bowerman, Pre's coach at Oregon, was one of the thousands who came away that evening with an even greater respect for the abilities of Steve Prefontaine.

"What the hell? Here's a guy that was going out of his depth, but he ran a great race. If Wottle had layed five yards off the pace, he'd have gotten whipped! Pre thrived on competition. That was one of the great things about the guy. To whip him, you almost had to be out of his class at the distance you were going to run. It never bothered him."

Summer in Europe

Three days after racing Wottle, Pre ran a 3:43.1 1500-meter in Helsinki, Finland. And one week after his Eugene race, he ran one of the most astonishing two-day doubles ever, in the World Games, again in Helsinki.

Ben Jipcho from Kenya had just raced to a new world record in the 3000-meter steeplechase in 8:14.0, and the spectators jammed into the Olympic Stadium were excited for more. The next race was the 5000, and Pre towed the field through the first 2000 meters, with Viren and Puttemans, two of his Olympic rivals, especially close. The crowd of 26,000 set up the rhythmic clapping and chanting that makes the adrenaline surge. Pre responded with 800 meters to go and started a long drive, but Puttemans, the world-record holder, had too much left and finished the last 200 in 26.0. Pre was second in a new American record of 13:22.4. Viren faded to fifth.

"I didn't realize the race was that fast," Pre said. "When he passed me, I let him go because I thought his kick would be too much. Had I known that the race was going to be this fast, I might have tried harder and I think I could have put up a much better fight. Now I want to stay in Finland and get into shape for some serious races."

Whether it was the call of competition or of the necessary dollar from the meet promoter, Steve raced again the next day in the 1500. Wottle was in the race, as well as future world-record holder Filbert Bayi of Tanzania, and 10 other world-class middle-distance men. Jipcho was there, like Pre, coming back from a tough race the day before.

Bayi made no contest of it, sprinting lap splits of 53.6, 58.0, and 60.6. But behind him came the fastest mass finish in history. Pre was 11th, second to last, his worst finish in any track race save one. But his time was 3:38.1, an Oregon school record and equal to a 3:55.5 mile. He had come back after his fastest 5000 ever to run faster than any of Oregon's many mile stars had ever run for 1500 meters.

Prefontaine then ran three quick, uninspired races in succession at non-AAU tour meets, most likely for financial reasons. Meet promoters routinely—and illegally—made "under-the-table" payments to stars like Prefontaine. These stars put people in the seats and always provided a good show. Sometimes the payment would be made in the form of a round-trip air ticket sent by each European meet, with the unused tickets cashed in by the athlete for a refund. Sometimes the payment would be made directly to the athlete by the promoter after the meet was over, always in U.S. dollars. A long line of tired athletes waiting outside the promoter's hotel room at midnight was a common sight. Everyone involved found it a demeaning exercise and damning proof of the hypocrisy of the amateur system.

Pre lost two 1500s, but won the 5000 at a meet in Oulu, Finland. Compared to his pre-Olympic tours, the act of winning did not seem to be as important as before. He was "putting in his time," as he phrased it, gaining international experience for future years.

It was fun traveling around with tour partners Ralph Mann and Dave Wottle, but by the middle of July and the U.S. match against Sweden and West Germany and his old nemesis Harald Norpoth, Pre was ailing. His troublesome sciatica was back, but so were Norpoth's recurrent stomach problems.

In the 5000-meter, Prefontaine ran the first 3000 in 8:02, and only the wraith-like Norpoth stuck closely. Then Pre had difficulty.

"It was at that point that I wanted to bear down and step up the pace," he said, "but I couldn't. I wasn't tired, but I couldn't go any faster. My race in the 5000 is in the last five laps, but when I'd start to move that last mile, my back would tighten up."

Norpoth outkicked Prefontaine over the last 200 for a

13:20.6 to 13:23.8 win. There were bigger rivals in Pre's career than the wily West German—Lasse Viren among them—but none whose racing style he detested more. "Anybody but him," Pre said. "I'll be back."

Upset by his physical problems, Pre cut short his tour and returned to the United States after one more 5000, a loss to the Belgian Puttemans at an international meet in Louvain, Belgium. The 1973 tour was less than Pre had hoped for, but during three of the races he had run the fastest 5000 of his life and set an American record, recorded the third-fastest 5000 ever by a U.S. athlete, and become the number nine American in the 1500. By now, however, he was thinking in terms larger than being the best American.

An Extra Season

Pre flew back to Eugene and resumed the lifestyle of the student-athlete on summer break. He drove new cars down to California to be sold and waited around until there was one going north.

He continued to train in preparation for the cross country season, an extra one he was granted after sitting out the 1972 fall season. He also readied himself for a final semester of classes before graduating with a degree in Broadcast Communications in the winter of 1973.

One day, shortly after his return from Europe and the galling defeat by Norpoth, a group of Oregon runners were out on a road run. One of them, Dave Taylor, is a runner of slender physique, much like Norpoth.

"Guys on the team used to give me a hard time about how I'm built," he explains, "so I had this T-shirt made up with 'NORPOTH' on the back.

"About halfway through the run, I whipped off my sweat-shirt and took off sprinting in front of Pre. He went into a rage, and came up and grabbed me and started choking me, and said, 'If that skinny sonuvabitch, if he ever does that to me again, here's what I'll do to him,' and here he was beating me up on the run. It was in fun and he was smiling, but he let us know that he didn't really appreciate what the guy had done."

Pre turned on the steam and left the pack behind en route to his 5000-meter heat victory at the 1972 U.S. Olympic Trials in Eugene, Oregon.

After a missed meeting earlier in the year, Pre finally got to challenge George Young, the 34-year-old former world-record holder in the two-mile, in the finals of the Olympic Trials 5000.

With two laps to go, Pre and Young have the race to themselves. With just over a lap to go, Pre took off on his way to an American record.

Steve receives the spoils of his Trials victory from track fan John Gillespie, now a University of Oregon assistant track coach.

Pre ran his victory laps wearing one of the gag T-shirts that were made in response to the "Go Pre" T-shirts.

"Everybody was around him, looking at him, but he wasn't aware of them. His eyes were totally open and not really smiling, but he had a kind of 'I did it' look. He was in another world."—Pat Tyson, Pre's roommate, commenting on Pre after his Trials 5000 victory.

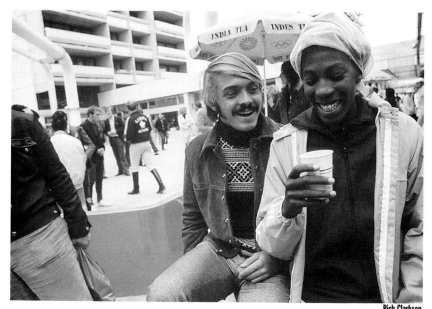

Rich Clarkson

Before the terrorist attack on the Israeli athletes at Munich in 1972, Steve hung out with other athletes in the Olympic Village. Here he is with Madeline Manning, an 800-meter runner for the U.S. team.

Don Chadez

Steve began his drive in the 1972 Olympic 5000 final as they approached the bell for the last lap. Twice he tried to pass Finland's Lasse Viren, and twice he was cut off by Mohamed Gamoudi of Tunisia (904).

On the last lap, Pre seemed to have a lock on a medal as he hung tight with Viren and Gamoudi.

Exhausted by his attempts for the gold, Pre staggered to a fourth-place finish behind Great Britain's Ian Stewart. "Give Prefontaine his due," Stewart said of the race. "The way I ran, I didn't deserve an Olympic medal."

Rich Clarkson

A devastated Pre wanted nothing to do with reporters after the Olympic 5000 final.

Rich Clarkson

Pre shared this trailer in the Glenwood area of Eugene, a few miles from Oregon's campus, with Pat Tyson from early 1972 to mid-1973.

A rare moment of relaxation. This photo was taken for a 1972 article on Pre in LIFE magazine.

Rich Clarkson

Pre's mother, Elfriede (to Steve's left, holding purse), father, Ray (far left, holding cushions), and sister Linda (white jacket) were among his biggest fans.

"Go Pre" T-shirts were a hot-selling item in stores throughout Eugene.

Pre-mania.

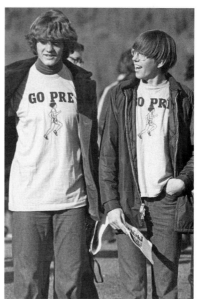

Jeff Johnson

Rich Clarkson

Steve would occasionally train on the sand dunes north of his hometown of Coos Bay.

Pre seemed to derive energy from the crowd's enthusiasm as he upset milers Marty Liquori and Henryk Szordikowski in the Los Angeles Times Indoor mile in February 1973.

The start of a rivalry. The press tagged Paul Geis (left) as Pre's "heir-apparent" after he transferred from Rice to Oregon during Pre's senior year.

An hour after winning the mile at a quadrangular meet in April 1973, Pre outlasted stubborn John Ngeno of Washington State in the three-mile for the best one-day double performance in world history.

Coach Bill Dellinger and Ngeno congratulate Pre after his incredible double victory.

Pre's hero status in Eugene rose even higher after he ran a 3:55.0 mile, the third-best performance in U.S. history, at the 1973 Oregon Twilight meet.

Despite troublesome sciatica, Pre "pulled every trick out of the hat, including making noises," to defeat John Ngeno of Washington State and the field in winning his fourth Pac-8 three-mile championship in May 1973.

Jeff Johnson

"It was a living legend that the clouds went away when Pre stepped on the track."—John Gillespie, track fan

In his last race as a collegian in front of the home fans, Pre edged Paul Geis by 0.2 second in the two-mile at the Oregon Twilight II meet.

1973 NCAA Championships, Baton Rouge, Louisiana: The scoreboard says it all. Pre smashed his own NCAA three-mile record by 13 seconds for his fourth consecutive championship.

Oregon doesn't run many meets during its cross country season. The goal is to emerge from the fall with a solid foundation for outdoor track, and a five- or six-mile race every weekend is more likely to tear the runner down than to build him up. It's not that the season is underemphasized, the coaches will tell you, it's just not overemphasized.

So when Pre met up with John Ngeno in the Northern Division race of the Pac-8, he may have been a tad short on races. Or, perhaps Ngeno was improving and Pre wasn't, the doubters said. In any case, Pre had to hustle to outsprint Ngeno at the tape by 0.8 second. Right then, the chances for a third Pac-8 cross country title looked in doubt.

But the next week in the Pac-8 meet at Stanford's golf course, it was the Pre of old. Tough, cagey, indomitable.

Through the flat first mile-and-a-half, Ngeno pulled Pre and Irishman Danny Murphy from Washington State free from the pack. Rain was making the going slippery, and at times the Kenyan's naturally skittish gait was close to sprinting as he windmilled around the turns and got 50 yards on Steve.

On the back three miles of cambered hills, Pre closed and caught Ngeno with two miles to go on the 5.9-mile course. He ran the fourth mile in 4:20 and finished by breaking the record he shared with Gerry Lindgren from four years before by a convincing 28 seconds.

"He just alternated the pace, and I love that kind of race," Pre exulted.

In the typical postrace crush of reporters and autograph seekers, someone asked the winner if he was looking forward to future races against young Craig Virgin from Illinois, who the summer before had broken Pre's two-mile high school mark by a half-second. The pride flared in Prefontaine.

"It's not a matter of me racing him; he has to come and race me!" Still irritated, Pre continued, "That's not much of a record-breaking performance—what, a half a second—no, I'm not impressed."

With two weeks to go before the NCAA Championships in Spokane, Washington, Prefontaine received continuous treatment on his back and trained as best he could. Despite his convincing win in the Pac-8 meet, his confidence was at an all-time low.

"We went to the NCAA championship meet in Spokane," Dave Taylor recalls, "and I'd never seen Pre act like he did there. He had injured his back and was really in a panic. He was a regular person at that meet—even locked himself in his room at 8:00 that night. Rose nearly got him."

Nick Rose of Western Kentucky had been running well that 1973 season. He came from the British blood-and-guts school of distance running, where you ran until you dropped. But he was also intelligent, and race-wise enough to have won the International Junior Cross Country match in 1970. Still, Prefontaine was Prefontaine, a fact of which Rose was aware.

"I had been running the way I run best," Rose says. "Just hammering for about four miles and then hanging on, and I thought that was what I was going to do."

By the halfway mark of the beautiful course, Rose had 50 yards on Pre and seemed to be gaining at each downhill stretch. The course was a loop, and on the second circuit, the pack behind could see the lead Rose held.

"I thought it was all over," exclaims Doug Brown, an Olympian in the steeplechase in Munich. "At three miles, Rose had a good 50 or 60 yards on him, and I thought, 'Wow, the race is over. Pre's gonna get beat—he might even come back to me!'"

Meanwhile, both of the front-runners were in a quandary. The pace was hurting Pre. He glanced back and saw that nobody was going to catch him for second, "so it was either do or die," he later told Taylor. So he went after Rose.

"It's strange," Rose muses. "I didn't really think that I was going to beat him. I knew that I had a big lead at one stage, but I just had this feeling . . . I was sort of waiting for the guy to come up and take me, and when he did, I had sort of given up a bit. Maybe if I had had more confidence. . . ."

With less than a mile to go, Pre pulled even, and once level, knew the race was in hand. Rose clung, then faded, and Prefontaine had his third cross country title, leading his Oregon team to an overwhelming victory in the team championship.

Buerkle's Turn

The 1974 indoor season started with the invitational CYO meet in College Park, Maryland. Pre had been training hard for three weeks to prepare for the two-mile race.

The field did not look overpowering, although Dick Buerkle, who had given Pre the struggle the year before in the AAU Championships, was in it. Pre led, as usual, through a 4:15 first mile, which broke him away from everyone but Buerkle. In fact, Dick moved into the lead past the mile.

"I wanted to challenge him, see what he had," Buerkle says.

With five laps to go on the 160-yard track, Buerkle moved out into lane two, but Pre could not assume the lead. "When I moved out, if he took off, then I'd just have had to stay with him, run a little harder," Buerkle states. "But when I moved out and he didn't do anything, then I knew it was mine. I went out and ran as hard as I could, and he didn't stay with me. I looked back with a half-mile to go, and he was hurting.

"I just moved out; it was my turn. He was tuckered out."

Buerkle's time was 8:26.2; Prefontaine's a still-good 8:33.2. It was his first loss to an American at a distance over a mile since the AAU Championships of 1970.

Pre shrugged off the defeat, but as one teammate recalls, "he worked his tail off when he got back to Eugene. He was super-pissed."

A week later, he won the two-mile at the Sunkist Invitational in Los Angeles in a time not much faster—8:33.0—but with no one within seven seconds of him. Buerkle was not in the race.

He continued to train hard, and with the defeat by Buerkle still fresh in his mind, his mental direction asserted itself. In fact, Pre's next race may have been his finest indoor race ever. Not because it was fast—it was, an American record 8:22.2 for the two-mile—or because it excited the fans—it didn't, as the Portland crowd of 8,000 present for the Oregon Invitational was strangely lackluster in its support. No, because this one race shows how much Pre could put his mind to running when he wanted to.

Dave Taylor, who was there, describes it well:

"Geis was in the race, and he and Pre had a little feud going. Geis took off from the gun and went through the half in about 2:04, and Pre was right behind him.

"Then something really strange happened: Pre took off at about the half, and all of a sudden he got so involved in the race that he basically went into a trance. I'll never see anyone run this fast again. He ran 61 for the next quarter and 2:03 for the next half. He came through the mile-and-a-half at world-record pace. And you could look in his eyes, and he was so involved I don't think he even realized where he was.

"Then somebody shouted at him, and he started looking around and slowed down, just like that. He just snapped out of it. I've always felt that if he'd gone another quarter before he snapped out of it, that would have been pretty awesome to see."

One month after his loss to Buerkle, Pre was now thoroughly in shape. Realizing this, he extended his indoor season to include the San Diego Indoor. In the two-mile race was New Zealander Dick Tayler, fresh off a 10,000-meter triumph in the Commonwealth Games the month before. Here indeed was worthy competition.

For awhile, it seemed like a typical Prefontaine indoor race—Steve doing all of the work, and everybody else hanging on for as long as possible. By the mile (4:09), only Tayler was with him, and they had a 40-yard gap on the field. Pre was running close to world-record pace, and he was beginning to feel it.

Suddenly, with six laps left, Tayler moved to the front.

"I realized by taking the lead so early, it might have cost me the race," Tayler explained later. "But I felt good and I wanted the screaming crowd to see a record. I knew we could do it."

Pre relaxed behind Tayler for four laps of San Diego's super-fast 160-yard oval, then sprinted by with two laps remaining for a two-second win in 8:20.4, the third-fastest in the world at that point, and another American record.

"Those people from overseas are much more generous that way," Pre commented about Tayler's pacesetting. "I wish more Americans were that way."The track felt great," Pre concluded, "but I didn't."

6
Hard Work

To attain and maintain the fitness of a world-class runner, three factors must be present: physical ability, mental tenacity, and plenty of hard work.

From those early years in Coos Bay, of sprinting between telephone poles and tacking up notes on his dresser to "Beat Doug Crooks" or some other rival, Pre had these factors in abundance. Later, surrounded by very good, even great runners at Oregon, he was nonetheless a step above, and everyone recognized it.

"There did seem to be a difference between Pre and the other runners," teammate Lars Kaupang of Norway says. "He seemed to be able to go out on the track and do three-quarter miles, half-miles, miles, all by himself, and he was able to push himself to a limit that nobody else could."

Training was not always all that much fun, as Pre himself admitted. "It really gets grim until the competition begins," he once said. "You have to wonder at times what you're doing out there. Over the years, I've given myself a thousand reasons to keep running, but it always comes back to where it started. It comes down to self-satisfaction and a sense of achievement."

Road Training

There were several unusual features to the Prefontaine training program. No matter what time he went to bed the night before, Pre was up the next morning at 6:00 A.M. and out the door at a six-minute-mile pace. He believed that any work done at a pace slower than that would not do him any good. Considering his abilities, he may have been right.

And while he certainly trained on the roads, Pre was not a road runner. He never ran road races and never pushed his daily road workouts. They were a means of building strength while recovering from some brutal afternoon track sessions. During the time they shared the trailer in Springfield in 1972–1973, Prefontaine and Pat Tyson often did their morning runs together.

"Whenever you went for a run with him, he would never let you know when he was going to turn," Tyson says. "He wouldn't warn you, in other words. Most runners are kind of polite and will signal when they're about to turn right or left, especially when you haven't been on that run before. But Pre would just cruise, and you would learn to keep a couple of yards behind him and watch very closely. He definitely led the workouts.

"Steve would always ask me, when we were on a run in the morning especially, 'How're you feeling? How're you feeling?' I think he was really concerned about how I felt, but I'd just say 'fine', even though sometimes I might have felt terrible.

"Pre didn't like to go on a run of more than 12 miles. Said he didn't enjoy running that much. He would max at about 10 miles. They were always at six-minute pace or faster. On Sundays, he might go out for an additional 4 to 5 miles in the afternoon real easy—excuse me, six-minute pace.

"The runs he'd pick were boring and repetitious— through Springfield by the railroad tracks, by industry. He always seemed to be fascinated by that. I'm sure he liked the trails, too. I never really analyzed it, but he may have wanted to be around more civilized things, so he ran through city streets. And he liked to stay away from hills."

On the roads for the easy days, Pre relaxed a bit and became less competitive. "That's where I really got to know him," teammate Mark Feig reflects, "on the roads, where we could talk. That's where I first learned of his warmth and where he was headed."

There was time to talk, trade jokes, and pull a few, too. Sometimes a guy nicknamed "Jack Frost" would tag along on the road workouts. He would rest up on the more intense training days, and then come out on the distance days to try to run with Pre. Eventually, it got to Steve, so one time he led Jack Frost up a deserted road in the woods, then sprinted back to the main group, leaving Jack to find his own way back to Eugene.

"There were some guys who just wanted to be able to say they had run with Pre," teammate Steve Bence says, "and he took care of them."

In the never-ending struggle against boredom, Pre wanted to run new routes. "All right, you guys decide where we're going to run," he would challenge Feig and Bence when they trained together on the roads. Feig would suggest the Bike Trail or Skinner's Butte, and Pre would respond with "That's not very original; everybody does that all the time."

"So we'd end up with him going off in the lead and end up running the same old thing we'd done before," Bence says.

To teammate Terry Williams, it sometimes seemed that Pre could have cared less where he was going on his runs. "Like one day, it was raining kind of hard. We have this cemetery right across from the gymnasium. He started out there—I thought we were going for a road run—but he just ran there. I followed him for 40 minutes in that cemetery, and he never did one full loop as we wandered around."

Serious Business

If the roads were a time of recovery and comradeship, the track was where he savaged his body. "When he was on the road, he just ran," Tyson says, "but he thrived on the track. On the track, he was in his own little world."

Pre would arrive at the Hayward Field track just before the start of the daily afternoon workout, and sometimes after it had started. A few laps of warmups, and he was ready to rip through the workout, tear it to pieces, and leave most of the Oregon team far behind in his wake. And unlike those who could manage several such workouts and then break down with illness or injury, Pre had the physique and temperament to come back for more.

"I guess the thing that stands out," says Oregon coach Bill

Dellinger quietly when asked of Pre's greatest talent, "is that he went through four years of college without ever missing a workout because of a cold or illness. Four years of never missing any meets.

"I always had the feeling that he was doing the same workouts, but basically expending about 70 percent energy on what were really tough workouts, whereas the other guys would be spending 90 percent."

Indeed, some of his workouts are the stuff of legend, like the one Bence calls Steve's "greatest."

"During the summer of 1974, Pre was preparing for a return trip to Europe. It was supposed to be 2 × 1-mile with a 5- to 10-minute slow jog between. Pre asked for some moral support, so we showed up to give him encouragement. His first mile was 4:08. Four seconds too fast. His second mile was supposed to be 4:08. We asked Pre how he expected to run his second mile as fast or faster. He responded by running 4:02.8."

Sometimes after the afternoon workout, Pre would stop by the weight room for 10 or 15 minutes of work, but it wasn't with the diligence he applied to running. His remarkable upper-body strength was partially an inherited gift and partially a result of the pull-ups he performed without fail. More important, he felt, were situps, for abdominal strength. Back from his morning run, Pre did numerous sets, and, in a typical timesaving measure, massaged his head at the same time, Tyson relates. "Pre was losing his hair, and he had been told that the secret to keeping it was to rub your scalp and take a lemon every day. I don't know if he took the lemon, but he'd rub his head to keep good circulation in there."

Combined with Pre's strength and resiliency was what is glibly termed "mental toughness." It was very real and he had plenty of it.

"Pre's biggest asset on the track was his competitive personality," teammate and rival Paul Geis states. There was a workout once where the team was supposed to run three 1320s in 3:20, 3:16, and 3:12. Scott Daggatt, one of the few runners who could stay with Pre over the long haul, ran 3:08 on the first one.

"He went with me and he was pissed," Daggatt notes. "Then we went 3:06. On the last one, he said, 'Goddamit, I'm going to do it to you, Daggatt.' He went 3:00 and I went 3:02."

"Pre had to be number one in workouts," Geis says. "I remember another time when Scott might have blown by him at one part of the workout. Three days later, Pre just obliterated him, and you realized what had happened: Pre had gone home and for the next 48 hours had mentally prepared his case.

"There were many casualties left in his wake of people trying to keep up with him, myself included."

7

End to Innocence

The spring of 1974 was Steve's first year as an "open" athlete, and there were difficult adjustments to make. He no longer had to contend with the collegiate dual-meet schedule, a man-killer of meets every weekend that Pre rarely coasted through. But then, he wasn't on show every weekend either and didn't have a conference or national meet to get ready for.

"I get the idea a lot of people think I died," Pre complained. "Sometimes people come up to me and ask me what I'm doing now."

He moved out of his trailer and into a house with Steve Bence and Mark Feig on Amazon Drive in Eugene for a few months, close to the Paddock Tavern, his favorite watering hole. Eventually, he was to move into a house that he bought on McKinley Street in Eugene, where he felt more settled and at home.

Now 23, Prefontaine still had that odd mixture of stubbornness and naïveté which marked his personality. When he first met teammate Steve Bence, who had attended an Air Force high school in Spain, Pre said he thought Bence spoke pretty good English for a Spaniard. And it hadn't been all that long since the time Prefontaine was out on an easy-day road run with then-freshmen Terry Williams, Dave Taylor, and several others. It was supposed to be a relaxed 10-miler, but one runner took off and disappeared, which nettled Pre to no small degree. So near the end of the run, when Taylor and Williams started to pick it up, it was too much for Pre. He caught up with the two of them, grabbed each by the shoulder and started screaming that there was no way they would ever make it, that they were both going to burn out so fast.

"Today it makes me laugh," Williams says, "and I understand what he was trying to get across, and he was right. But he just didn't know how to explain it to us, so he jumped on us—literally!"

That fierce energy, the man of action in Prefontaine, was something to behold. "Whenever Pre stayed with Feig and me," Bence says, "I could have sworn that he was living on five or six hours of sleep a night. Pre generally got in after midnight and before Mark or I was awake in the morning, he had run, showered, and eaten breakfast.

"Pre said at that time he was going to grow a garden at his new house on McKinley. I thought that he would never have the time to work on it, but I was wrong," Bence admits. "It wasn't long until his salads included vegetables from his back yard."

In addition to his nontrack activities, Steve was getting in two workouts a day and running up to 100 miles a week. Near the end of April, after a few low-key tune-up meets, he was ready to tackle his first serious outdoor race of 1974 at the Oregon Twilight meet.

"I haven't done the quality work to run a good mile," Pre noted. He asked the Twilight meet organizers to add a 10,000-meter race rather than a six-mile. The metric distances were not run very much in the United States at that time. Most of the world, though, ran meters, the Olympic races were in meters, and a fast race at 10 kilometers would be of much more significance to Pre's competitors than one at six miles.

Olympic steeplechaser Mike Manley led through the mile, and then Pre took off on one of his loneliest races ever. The 7,000 fans who showed up in the chilly weather kept up steady encouragement, but as he clicked off the miles between 4:28 and 4:30, Pre was by himself. He sprinted the last lap in 58 seconds and won in an American record of 27:43.6.

"I could have gotten the six-mile world record today if I would have sprinted the last lap of it," Pre stated after his race.

Indeed, if he had run his 58-second lap at the finish of a six-mile, he would have beaten Ron Clarke's world mark by two seconds. And this was only Pre's second serious long race ever. As it was, his 27:43.6 was the sixth-fastest 10,000 ever run.

"I think this indicates I'm ready," he said with understatement. "And I still think I can run three miles with anybody in the world, including Paul Geis. I needed this one to compare with the Europeans. Now I'm shooting for bigger things."

The Lure of Big Money

The pressures of being out of college began to get to Pre. He now competed for the Eugene-based Oregon Track Club, but received no compensation. Even the paltry $101 per month scholarship for room and board he had received in college was money sorely missed. Some help came when he was hired after graduation by fledgling Nike. This association was a natural fit between the shoe company with Oregon roots and America's most popular track athlete. Pre's job description: National Public Relations Manager.

"I think he made up the title himself," recalls Geoff Hollister, a former Oregon distance runner who scheduled Pre, decathlete Jeff Bannister, discus thrower Mac Wilkins, and other athletes for clinics and public appearances. In typical fashion, Steve had business cards made up with his new title and threw himself into the job. After the then unknown Bill Rodgers placed third in the World Cross Country Championships in Rabat, Morocco, Pre sent him a letter and free shoes. Rodgers wore the shoes when he won his first Boston Marathon in 1975.

Steve did numerous running clinics for kids, worked the floor of the first Nike retail store, and learned what went into making shoes. For this, he received $5,000 per year, at the time strictly against the rules for an amateur athlete.

"Quite simply, we felt it was the right thing to do," Hollister says. "The idea was that Steve should have this as a training stipend, and it was not a lot to live off of, but it was going to make it easier for him."

It wasn't long before Pre again crossed swords with his old nemesis, the Amateur Athletic Union, track's governing body and upholder of the rules of "amateurism." In May 1974, he was sent a letter from the Chairman of the AAU Registration Committee informing him that the AAU national office had "received a report stating you have been wearing a sweat suit with the word "NIKE" on it. I believe you are aware, as I am, that by wearing this garment you are jeopardizing your amateur eligibility and future competition." Pre was to be supplied with a "proper sweat suit" by Nike, without the offending logo on it.

For Pre, it was one more vexation, one more shove in the direction of professional track and field. After the 1972 Olympics, the International Track Association (ITA) had been formed with the goal of establishing a pro circuit in the United States and, eventually, around the world. Former Olympic stars Kip Keino from Kenya, Jim Ryun, Bob Seagren, and others signed on; and the ITA meets drew reasonably well in the first year. But to sustain interest, the pro circuit needed a current star, a guaranteed draw, a showman. Quite simply, it needed Pre.

He was sorely tempted. His hand-to-mouth existence was frustrating for a go-getter like Pre. The ITA kept upping its offer all during 1974, until it approached $100,000 a year. This was substantially more than even the marquee athletes like Prefontaine earned in under-the-table payments common at the time in "shamateur" track. To turn pro would bring everything out in the open, above-board. "I just have to decide whether I want to make running a job and accept the responsibilities that go with it," Pre said.

To go professional would of course mean giving up a chance for a medal at the 1976 Olympic Games in Montreal. Throughout 1974, Pre engaged in an almost love-hate relationship with the entire concept of the Olympics. On the one hand, he was disillusioned by his experiences in Munich and the ongoing threat of boycotts of the Montreal Games over political issues. (Most of the African nations did boycott in 1976 in protest of a trip by a New Zealand rugby team to South Africa, which was banned at the time from Olympic competition because of its racial policies.) On the other hand, winning an Olympic medal, along with setting world records, were the greatest accomplishments possible for any track and field athlete. To an achiever like Prefontaine, it was the supreme challenge, and not one to be dismissed without long soul-searching.

Accepting the ITA offer would also mean the curtailment of several off-the-track projects he was pursuing. Foremost would be his evolving position as Nike's public relations manager. Athletes who remained amateurs would never be allowed to have business dealings with a professional athlete. To receive even a free pair of shoes from an ITA athlete would be to risk lifetime banishment from the sport.

Pre had also given serious thought to opening a sports bar in Eugene or Springfield with the name "Sub-4," which would have pictures on its walls of all the Oregon milers who had broken four minutes. Its menu would specialize in Prefontaine favorites—fresh tossed salads and beer.

And Pre was involved with Hollister and Bannister in what they termed the "Decathlon Club." "When we'd go out and do the clinics, we were in touch with a lot of people who were interested in fitness," Hollister remembers. "People had a need for information and some kind of an organized program." The three envisioned opening a fitness club near Alton Baker Park in Eugene. It would have a wood-chip jogging trail close by, like those Pre had seen in Scandinavia, and would offer a variety of activities, not just running. Steve had kept detailed notes about all the training centers he had visited in Europe, their programs, fees, and design. Once again, however, bureaucracy intervened. Long months were spent lobbying the Parks Advisory Committee, and it kept tabling the proposal to make the land available for the Decathlon Club. Pre was getting increasingly irritated and frustrated. He had had enough of bureaucracies.

While pondering the choice between professional and amateur track, Pre spent most of his spare hours, briefcase in hand, going to classrooms, playgrounds, and recreational centers and interacting with the kids on many different levels.

Geoff Hollister's sister, Laura, worked as the secretary of the Decathlon Club and did some of the scheduling for his public appearances.

On Pre: Don Kardong

I can remember responding very viscerally when Pre was speaking about the difficulty of trying to be a world-class athlete in an amateur sport. I have always felt that when we finally began to move toward professionalism in the early 1980s, that his comments and strong feelings about that were on everyone's minds, especially mine.

I guess he was one of the first runners I remember saying, "How am I supposed to pay the bills, when somebody keeps telling me that I can't take any money?" He was the first person I ever heard trumpet these ideas.

I never thought I would be running past college. It's not a career path I ever chose. I'm sure to a large degree that excitement that Pre used to create has sent me down this path. It was just so exciting to be in the races he was in, and the way that people related to him. And the state of the sport at that period of time was so powerful and so much fun that all of that got me to stay in it, to make the Olympic team. And then here I am still at it, because it is hard to leave.

Don Kardong is a writer and a founder of the Association of Road Racing Athletes. He placed fourth in the 1976 Olympic Marathon.

"He always walked in and out of the office with a lot of speed and bounce," she recalls. "Sometimes he looked so serious but would break a big smile when he saw a friend. About this time he was really being recruited hard for pro track. Half the time he would say he was thinking about quitting track completely so he could work full-time and make good money. The other half of the time he would say he couldn't stop running and 'if I was in pro track, I would be getting paid for all my public appearances.'

"Once I asked, was he going to do it, turn pro? 'No, probably not,' he said. Sometimes he was really thinking about quitting. He had spent so much of his time running. He didn't want to be 'like an old football player who could never die,' he said. He wanted more than a good track record out of his life. He wanted people to know there was more to him than that. That he was intelligent and hard-working and creative. Not that he drank lots of beer and was on an ego trip. He wanted to give the people of Eugene—'My People'—more. When he thought about quitting track or turning pro, he thought about his people and how much support they had given him and he didn't want to let them down, ever. So he would keep running, until the Olympics at least. That was his decision. No pro track."

Pre continued to consider the offers from the ITA throughout the year, but friends slowly began to notice a renewed enthusiasm for running-related goals that to some extent had been missing since Munich. While he was never again to be enamored of the Olympic Games themselves, he gradually spoke more about competing in Montreal and said that his goal was *a* medal, not *the* medal. That would have been an almost-impossible concession for the Steve Prefontaine of 1972. This was the Pre of 1974. Older, more mature, and once again looking ahead to all of his options, within the sport and beyond.

Europe on the Horizon

This outdoor season was to be the "Year of Europe" for Prefontaine. Although by any standards but his own, he had acquitted himself well in his European tours since his graduation from Marshfield High, Steve was tired of being asked why he could win in Eugene but not in Europe. He was also tired of explaining that for the American collegiate athlete, you peaked in June, not in August like the Europeans. With his NCAA career now completed, Pre could finally train with the late-summer European track season in mind

"I'm really excited about getting to Europe healthy and fresh this summer," he said. "When I run a race this year, I want to be ready for it."

The first major competition of his European-style season was a three-mile at the Hayward Restoration meet in early June. Frank Shorter, winner of the gold medal in the 1972 Olympic Marathon, would be in the race; and in a decision that would eventually bring him once again into conflict with the governing bureaucracy, Pre chose to skip the AAU Championships to prepare. To the AAU, not only had the sport's top draw snubbed its biggest meet, but Pre's non-appearance meant he would not be on any international teams. He would, in effect, be traveling around Europe as a free agent. The moguls at "AAU House," as the national office in Indianapolis was called, were definitely not pleased.

But for Steve, their disapproval was inconsequential. He had other things to worry about. An unusual bout with the flu left him uncertain of his form, and preparation for the race against Shorter took priority.

"I haven't had a decent workout in about three weeks," he lamented, "and that may affect my confidence." Two low-key two-mile races in the mid-8:30s after his American-record 10,000 had done little to bolster that confidence. Nevertheless, he cut down on his workouts the week before the race and prepared for a fast pace.

On June 8, some of the best open athletes began warming up before a packed house in Eugene. As Rick Wohlhuter from the University of Chicago Track Club was running 880 yards in a world-record 1:44.1, Prefontaine checked in with Larry Standifer at the trainer's tent.

"Before his many big races, he would come in with a complaint of some kind," the Oregon trainer remembers. "A sore foot, tight hamstring, or any other mild complaint. I would always check him over, decide what the problem was, and we would treat it. Usually, it was of a mild nature. Steve was like a finely tuned machine, and if it wasn't running exactly right, he would know it."

Pre warmed up with Shorter and they exchanged thoughts about race goals. "There was an understanding between us that we would go together sharing the lead until a half-mile to go, and then whoever won, won," Shorter says. "But the object was to run under 13:00."

Working together, Pre and Shorter dropped the good field after a mile in 4:16.5, just a second off world-record pace.

Through nine laps in 9:44, the agreement worked; then Pre led for two straight.

"I don't think Frank held up his part of the bargain toward the end of the race," Pre groused later.

They had entered the stage of fast races where the protests of the body overrule the willingness of the mind. Then Shorter gathered, and with a quarter-mile remaining, shot into the lead.

The din, already awesome, increased in volume. Don Kardong, running alone in third place, had never heard anything like it. "I almost stopped," he says, "because it was really loud, and they weren't even watching me. The fans were pounding those wooden stands and shouting—beyond exciting, so loud, it was unnerving."

Into the backstretch, and all eyes were on Shorter and Pre and the 10-yard gap between them. They approached the last bend with the outcome still very much in doubt. Shorter, however, could feel himself tighten.

"When I started sprinting in the last 220, I knew I was dying, and I knew that I was going to go into the wind up the homestretch. So I thought that if he had anything left, he was probably going to get me."

Pre sensed the break. "I knew I had a chance with a 220 to go," he remarked. "I just relaxed, felt fresh again, and started accelerating."

Shorter was far from giving up, "but it was just a situation where you're going as hard as you can and that's it—there's nothing more there. I thought if I could get within 30 yards of the finish I could get him, because he tended to die a little bit in the last 10 to 15 yards. He caught me well before that, about 80 yards out."

Pre was running one of his fastest finishes ever, regardless of the length of the race, and he pulled ahead to win by 0.6 second in an American record of 12:51.4.

Years later, Shorter had this to say about the race: "I was trying to beat him, I can assure you of that. But Pre was the favorite son, and that was probably the difference. When I think of Oregon, I think of the homesteader mentality: tough, hard-nosed, direct. That was Pre. You cheered for him, you knew you'd get something in return."

As they warmed down together, Steve's fans offered congratulations to them both. One friend down on the crowded infield asked, "What happened out there? I thought you slowed down." Pre said, "Yeah, I almost let him win. I was just thinking it wasn't that big a deal. Then, I don't know, something inside of me just said, 'Hey, wait a minute, I want to beat him,' and I just took off!"

Later, when the reporters asked how he had pulled it out, Pre's answer encapsulated the strength he received from racing in Eugene.

"The idea of losing the three at Hayward Field and the idea of losing my specialty to someone who wasn't running his specialty. Mostly, the idea of losing in front of my people. They haven't forgotten about me."

8

Pre and His People

It was a unique love affair that the people of Coos Bay and Eugene had with Steve Prefontaine, and he with them. The intense loyalty he felt to his origins and his adopted community, combined with a prodigious talent and natural flamboyance, produced a personality that the two towns proudly came to cheer and embrace.

"That man has something no runner in my time had," Bill Dellinger once mused to Kenny Moore of *Sports Illustrated*. "We used to warm up out of sight behind the stands, and we would never have considered taking a victory lap. But Pre . . . he's almost like a movie star in his relationship with the crowd. He thrives on it."

For "His People," the feeling was mystical. "The last laps of his races were the most exciting moments I've ever experienced in viewing sports," is how one of Steve's fans summarized the feeling.

"The crowd was always on its feet, the excitement generated was riotous. The race was a victory for 'Pre's People' as much as for the runner himself. There will never be another sound like 'Go Pre!' There is no way the people of Eugene will ever forget Steve."

The feeling was there in Coos Bay, both during Steve's high school days and later, when he returned to visit. In the words of sportswriter Kenn Hess, who chronicled Pre's high school career for the *Coos Bay World*, the familiar refrain around the town at the time was, "'There goes Pre,' as he ran by along the highway, through the park or across the playgrounds during seemingly endless workouts. He attracted admiration, if not some awe."

And when he visited the town in later years of greater fame, "he always had a few moments for friendly chitchat. He almost always seemed to steer a conversation to 'how are you doing and what's new with you,' and seemed to prefer not to talk about himself or his latest exploit or disappointment. He was grassroots when he came home to see his parents and to visit."

His fame was welcomed by the town, as evidenced by the local movie theater owner who put "Go Pre" vanity license plates on his car, and by the all-weather track that, but for Pre, would still be cinders. And nearly everyone who ever met him, in either Coos Bay or Eugene or elsewhere, has some vignette, some story that for them typifies Steve Prefontaine.

In Their Voices

I was down at the AAU Championships in 1969 in Miami. I had arrived four or five days early and was down in the dorms where the athletes were staying. And I noticed this—well, I would have called him a very young, little, high school kid hanging around Lindgren and Bacheler, like a groupie.

One afternoon, I had just gotten in the elevator, and just as the door was closing, this little thing squirts in the door. It was that kid! He says, 'What do you do?' And I said, 'I don't do anything; I just take pictures for *Track & Field News*.' 'Oh yeah, what's your name? Oh yeah, I've heard of you.' I didn't see him again until he was down at the starting line for the three-mile.

From that first meeting, no matter what the race in later years—he'd be warming up for a big one, and he had a lot of them—he would come jogging by and always give me a little wink and a wave and then go on about his business.

—*Jeff Johnson, photographer*

Author's Note: At the 1972 Olympic Trials in Eugene, an event that was widely misinterpreted at the time was the so-called "T-shirt Incident." A group of track fans revealed shirts with a "Stop Pre" logo on them just before the start of the 5000 final. John Auka and John Gillespie, two of the instigators, between them saw nearly every race Pre ever ran in Eugene.

It was really done in fun because face it, John and I thought Prefontaine was the greatest thing in the world. I went down to Penney's and bought 30 of their best T-shirts. We thought we would top the "Go Pre" shirts that were being sold. The first person to be seen with one on was Gerry Lindgren, when he was running a warm-up lap. He sprinted around in his stop sign. Then a group of about 10 of us took off our shirts at once to expose the "Stop Pre" T-shirts on underneath. Several of the people around us muttered some unkind things when they realized what the shirts said.

Pre won in a cakewalk, of course. And after he started his victory lap and got halfway around, Gillespie ripped off his "Stop Pre" T-shirt and started waving it at Pre, who looked at it and kind of pointed to himself with a quizzical look on his face. And John said, "Yes, yes," and Pre put on the shirt and finished his victory lap.

Some people missed the point that it was all in fun, but Pre didn't.

—John Auka, track fan

That summer morning [in 1973], after my legs and lungs had burned out trying to copy Pre's style, he stopped and we chatted. We talked briefly of our dogs. We talked of food stamps, a student's best friend and something we were grateful to have. We talked of profs in the school of journalism who gave us more trouble than we thought we deserved.

Part of the attraction for Pre was that he was a regular guy. He drove a tacky old Ford station wagon. He took his dog to class. And on Friday afternoons, you'd see him quaffing beer at one of the slick bars off campus, like Duffy's or the Paddock, a favorite ritual for most of us. They'd give him all the beer he could drink, which was considerable, to pour a little beer, or to check ID, or to stand around and talk to other beer drinkers.

He was celebrated. He was loved. And he was one of the guys.

The first time I asked Pre for an interview, I was just starting as a sportswriter for the *Daily Emerald*, the University of Oregon student newspaper. He said no, he was far too busy. Listen, I said, I need to get this story, Steve, it's important. He said he'd give me an interview because I called him Steve. He got tired of everybody calling him Pre.

"Some people create with words or with music or with a brush and paints," he said. "I like to make something beautiful. When I run, I like to make people stop and say, 'I've never seen anyone run like that before.' It's more than just a race, it's style. It's doing something better than anyone else. It's being creative."

If you ever saw Pre run, you're lucky. The sight of him rounding the last turn and looking up at the clock will be forever frozen in my memory. The same is true of the way he scratched my dog's ears and muttered the silly things people say to dogs.

—*Don Chapman, former sports editor,* East Oregonian

I remember the only time I talked to him for any length was at the Munich Sheraton in 1973 on a big tour. I remember he talked about himself an awful lot—I was surprised. I thought he'd be a lot more formal. He told me that he didn't speak much English until he was five years old because his Mom was from Germany. He talked about his family a little bit, about his plans for the future, just small-talk things. It surprised me that he was as open and talked as easily as he did. I had expected him to be a big dynamic personality that you almost couldn't get next to.

—*Dick Buerkle, Olympian*

It was always like, 'Hey, there's a party going on,' when you met him. He'd say, 'Hey Macker, how are you?' He always called me Macker for some reason. "Hey you got to come; it'll be great," and so on. Really friendly and warm, and then, "Got to get going, see you later!"

I couldn't understand why when one of the best-looking

girls on campus would come up and ask him for a date two weeks down the road, he'd say, "Well, I don't know, I have to check my schedule." But basically, all this behavior that may have been abrasive or seemed cocky was just him being focused and honest.

—*Mac Wilkins, Oregon teammate and 1976 Olympic discus gold medalist*

Was he more subdued in Europe? Not when I was with him, he wasn't. I think maybe I saw him not subdued a few times over there. Perhaps he was on the average more subdued, but he was definitely not subdued.

—*Al Feuerbach, former world-record holder in the shot put, and a party companion*

In March 1974, we held a benefit dinner for a 14-year-old boy who had lost his left leg in a motorcycle accident. When Steve Prefontaine arrived, he was instantly surrounded by kids and responded to them beautifully.

After talking with the kids, he asked if he could be of any help. Since the gym activities were already well-staffed, he asked if he could help dish up the spaghetti dinners. Serve he did—for the rest of the day!

—*Jane Fleener, Eugene resident*

He liked to build things and use his hands. In the winter of 1974–1975, he built a sauna in his garage. Similar to those he'd used in Finland. And let me tell you this was an A-1 job. He was also very pleased with his garden every summer. These are things he was very proud of and things he planned on getting into after he retired. Steve was always talking about the future after running. They were always different, one week maybe working for a friend in some business or the next week buying a lot of land and being a farmer. But one thing he said he'd do was win the gold medal at Montreal.

—*Mark Feig, Oregon teammate*

My son was so inspired by Steve, and he ran for Springfield High School. If Steve could make it, and he usually did, he'd come to watch my son Dan run in the dual meets. He'd be on the track yelling his head off encouraging Dan. My son's running paid off. He joined the Army and became a member of the U.S. Modern Pentathlon team. If it hadn't been for Steve, I'm sure things would be different. But then Steve encouraged many, many kids.

—*Dee Williams, Pre's cousin*

It also bothered him when he was accused of not supporting women's track. Pre was very knowledgeable about women's track and was a great supporter. Even with his busy schedule, Pre found the time to write workouts and time a couple of the better women runners in Eugene.

All this criticism came about after a reporter asked Pre if he thought that the women's times were catching up with the men's. Pre's response was that his average mile time for six miles was faster than the women's American mile record. Women still had a ways to go. That prompted some women to write calling Pre a male chauvinist. He tacked up the letter with the strongest language on his kitchen bulletin board. Even though he laughed about it and called her ignorant, he seemed concerned that there might be others who misunderstood his meaning.

—*Steve Bence, Oregon teammate*

Whenever there was a chance, Pre and I would run and train together. During that time, I sensed a closeness as we would share sweat and conversation. I particularly enjoyed Pre's lack of shyness. If I signed an autograph "Go with God," he'd ask why. Very few people ask why. Pre was that unique person who wanted to know and would not take things for granted.

—*Jim Ryun, former mile world-record holder*

He had charisma. That word—there's something about somebody when you tell people you're going to do something, and then you go out and do it. I know of no single person who could draw people like he did. You could have had a high school meet, and if you announced Pre was running, you'd have an overflow crowd. The Eugene people really admired his gutsiness.

No matter what the race . . . my Lord! The 1500 he ran against Hailu Ebba was the greatest race he ever ran. You talk about gutsy—there was no way Pre could have lost that. What I'm saying is—Steve Prefontaine, there in Eugene— you could just feel the strength of the crowd go into him.

It was a living legend that the clouds went away when Pre stepped on the track. It's really true. The track meet would be going, and Pre would jog into the stadium, and in the first place, everybody would start applauding him. The minute he took a step on it, the clouds would start . . . clearing up. The sun would shine through. It sounds funny, but I can remember just offhand four or five times, and I'm guessing there must have been more. I can remember people turning to somebody else and saying, "It's doing it again."

—*John Gillespie, coach and fan*

He just had whatever that is—I don't know, actors have it. Singers have it. Some people have it, some people don't. Most people don't. He had a lot of it.

—*Wendy Ray, Hayward Field announcer for all of Pre's races there*

9
Europe

"Europe" to the American athlete of the 1970s was a word full of promise. It meant late-night flights, little training time, and jammed racing schedules. It also meant good times, new friends, and track crowds of a size rarely seen in the United States.

In Scandinavia, especially, summer was a time for every small town to promote a meet, bring in some of the world's best athletes, and watch great track and field. It perhaps could only happen in cultures where professional sports do not monopolize the spectator dollar—in any case, it still makes Europe the meeting place of the world's track and field athletes.

Ten days after the Hayward Restoration meet, Pre ran his first race in Europe for the 1974 season. It was a 3000-meter in Tampere, Finland, against Olympic 1500-winner Pekka Vasala. Pre planned a six-week tour, most of it in Finland, with occasional junkets to Sweden and any other countries that could make it worth his while. In this race, he showed no signs of jet lag, winning by over four seconds in a solid 7:55.8. It was a good beginning to a tour on which he averaged a meet nearly every third day.

The first important 5000 of the tour was eight days later, at the World Games in Helsinki, Finland. At a glance, the participants looked like they might have been transported from an Oregon Twilight meet of a year or two before: besides Pre, Paul Geis was there, as well as Oregon grads Arne and Knut Kvalheim of Norway.

Good friend Mark Feig set off at an ambitious pace and led through the first kilometer, where Pre took over. He pressed through a fast 3000 in 8:03.2, with Knut Kvalheim shadowing him, looking far better than he had in the Restoration meet where he'd finished fourth.

"By the end of June, Knut had done some excellent workouts," Oregon teammate Lars Kaupang notes, "like 2 × 1500 in 3:45 with four minutes rest. So Knut knew he was ready."

At the bell lap, Pre still led, but on the backstretch with 300 meters to go, Kvalheim sprinted. Pre tried to respond, to gather as he had against Shorter 18 days before, but Kvalheim was too strong. Thirty meters from the tape, Prefontaine dropped his arms in defeat and coasted across the line, in a personal best and American record of 13:21.9, but 1.4 seconds behind Kvalheim. Pre had run the fastest 5000 he would ever run and had finished second over his distance to a teammate who had never before beaten him.

"I was tired," Pre said later. "I wasn't competitive. We were neck and neck with 50 yards left, but suddenly I thought, 'Oh hell, I don't want this bad enough. I don't care. Take it.'"

Of that race, Geis remembers Kvalheim's joy at finally beating Prefontaine. "He said, 'I've waited four years for this moment!' I think he had."

Pre then traveled to Italy, for an international meet in Milan—and again lost while running better than any American had before. His 7:42.6 in the 3000 lost out to New Zealander Rod Dixon's 7:41.0. Skipping the big Bislett Games in Oslo, Norway, Pre retreated to Finland to take stock. Mentally, he was not in Europe to lose, and defeat was difficult to handle. Sure, he liked to party and have a good time, but this trip, his main goal was to win.

"I think as soon as he lost once, he had problems getting back," Kaupang suggests. "He started to think he was out of shape or that he was injured. He was so used to running by himself and breaking everybody else in Eugene. Then he would be over in Europe and realize that with a lap to go, there were maybe five or six guys on his heels. That's kind of tough on a runner's mind when you're so used to being able to break everybody."

Pre trained hard in Finland. He cut down on his beer consumption and got 10 hours of sleep a night. He tried to rest his sore back as much as possible. Nevertheless, as Ralph Mann remembers, there was time for a little fun.

"There was nothing else to do where we were staying in the northern part of Finland but take saunas and eat the local food. So Pre, Dave Wottle, and I got together, and the mayor of this little town printed up some posters, and we had a track meet—the three of us against the whole town. It was quite an event."

After two weeks of training, Pre met Dixon again in a two-mile at the July Games in Stockholm, at that time an annual event in Sweden. When Pre stepped out on the track, he was given a particularly warm reception. The Scandinavian crowds liked his fearless front-running, and it was not unusual for the spectators to take up the chant of "Pre! Pre!," much as they would have for a Lasse Viren or national hero Anders Garderud.

"They loved his style," states Feig, who traveled with Pre on the 1974 tour, "the guy who will lead and force the pace. They dug it."

This was truly a fast field, with Dixon, Emiel Puttemans of Belgium, Jos Hermens of the Netherlands, Dick Buerkle, Geis, Marty Liquori, and Suleiman Nyambui of Tanzania in the race. Buerkle finished fifth in a personal best of 8:24.2, but what he remembers is that the crowd expected Pre to set the pace.

"And he went out and did it—played into people's hands. It was kind of like a challenge: 'I'm going to run as hard as I can and beat everybody.' They knew if he was in the race, it was going to be a good race and an exciting race. Anytime Pre ran, it was going to be a fast time. He did not run just to win."

Prefontaine set out to grind his opponents into the track. Many of them did drop, but with a lap to go, a pack was still with him, and he was helpless to stop Dixon and Puttemans from sprinting on by.

"It was so weird," Feig remarks, "because I've seen him run a three-mile or two-mile and he'd kick the last lap in like

58 seconds. And he ran the last lap in 58 in that thing, but they ran 55. Mowed him down in the last 110.

"And when they passed him, he just quit. He'd led the whole thing until the last 100 yards, but once they got by him, he was through. He was so pissed, he went out and *got* pissed."

Pre was a well-beaten third, in 8:18.4 to Dixon's 8:14.4. Once again, he had run faster than any American ever had, and had forced his opponents to run their best: Dixon set a New Zealand record.

Pre was still short of his primary goal, however—to win. At age 23, he was gaining strength and getting faster, as his American records at every distance from 3000 to 10,000 showed, but the fantastic Eugene winning streak couldn't be continued once he went against the cream of the world's distance runners. Those who saw him in both the United States and Europe have varying opinions why.

"Prefontaine was tough every time he went out," Liquori states unequivocally. "The only drawback he had as a runner was that his last 100 yards wasn't in the same class as a Viren or Great Britain's Brendan Foster. I think that was the only thing that held him back in the 5000. I think he would have had more potential in the 10,000 because his tactic of running away from people would have worked better."

In a way, Paul Geis says, Pre's nature wouldn't let him run a race like most of the Europeans did it: hang with the leader, conserve energy, and kick like mad over the last lap. "He was so hyper, he'd start getting scared in a race. So he'd take the pace and really push it. He wouldn't sit back and wait. He wasn't a gambler in that respect. He wouldn't take that kind of risk."

But both Geis and Lars Kaupang think Pre would have performed even better than he did if American track had the same schedule as the European season with its late-summer peak.

"I just think that he always had a pretty tough season over in the United States," says Kaupang. "He had super races all of the time and was racing nearly every weekend. Then he went over to Europe and most Europeans were just getting

Jeff Johnson

1973 NCAA Cross Country Championships, Spokane, Washington: Nick Rose of Western Kentucky led by 50 yards over Pre halfway through the six-mile course, but with a mile to go, Pre passed him. Pre was granted an extra season of eligibility because he did not compete in the fall of 1972.

Rose clung but eventually faded, resulting in Pre's third NCAA cross country title.

Jeff Johnson

1973 NCAA Cross Country team champions. Standing, left to right: Bill Dellinger, Dave Taylor, Gary Barger, Randy James, Scott Daggatt, Bill Bowerman. Kneeling, left to right: Terry Williams, Steve Prefontaine, Tom Hale.

"It was my turn."—Dick Buerkle, after winning the 1974 CYO two-mile. It was Pre's first defeat over a mile to an American since the summer of 1970.

Pre and his former coach, Bill Bowerman, at the 1973 opening of the first Nike retail store, called The Athletic Department and located in Eugene, Oregon.

Pre's finest indoor race ever, the 1974 Oregon Invitational in Portland. He seemed to be in a world of his own as he set an American record in the two-mile.

Erik Hill

Steve and Frank Shorter (left) alternated the lead during the 1974 Hayward Restoration three-mile in Eugene, Oregon, while Knut Kvalheim and Don Kardong tried to hang on. Steve won and set an American record.

Erik Hill

Pre joined Oregon Track Club teammates and other local runners in Eugene's first international-style cross country race in the fall of 1974.

Erik Hill

In September 1974, Pre thanked 1,000 fans who watched him run a 3:58.3 "tune up" mile in preparation for his return to Europe. Smoke from farmers burning ground cover caused him to cough blood after the race.

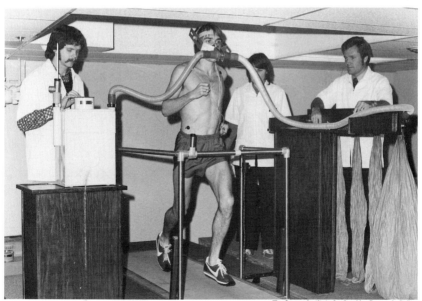

The Cooper Institute for Aerobics Research; Dallas

America's best distance runners were subjected to a battery of psychological and physiological tests at the Institute for Aerobics Research in Dallas in January 1975. Pre's test results placed him near the top of the world's elite athletes.

Pre took on the steepest street in Los Angeles before the 1975 Sunkist Invitational indoor meet.

Former Oregon distance runner Geoff Hollister scheduled Prefontaine and other athletes for public appearances and clinics.

Knowing he was not in top form, Pre looked suitably grim as he lined up with Rod Dixon (hands in air), John Walker, and Filbert Bayi (far right) for the Los Angeles Times mile in February 1975. Pre finished fifth, his worst indoor placing since high school.

Among Pre's many interests, one of his favorites was holding running clinics for his young fans.

Steve, relaxed and happy, chatted with friend Frank Shorter before the start of his last race on May 29, 1975.

Erik Hill

With three laps to go in his last 5000, Pre forced the pace against Shorter.

In his last victory, Pre's winning streak at distances over a mile in Eugene was extended to 25.

Erik Hill

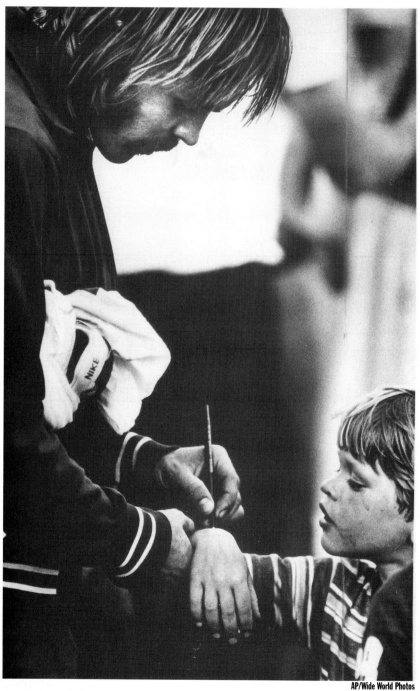

"Best Wishes—Pre"

Erik Hill

Moments before the last victory lap in front of his fans.

AP/Wide World Photos

Three days after his last race, fellow track athletes served as pallbearers at Pre's funeral at Pirate Stadium in Coos Bay.

Don Chadez

The crash site became an instant memorial.

Gary Dobbs

Twenty years after his death, mementos are still placed at "Pre's Rock."

Geoff Parks

"When you are a young and up-and-coming runner in the U.S., and making some breakthroughs in distances, Pre is still the man that you are compared to. It's always based on Pre."—Bob Kennedy, American-record holder at 3000 and 5000 meters, in a 1995 article by Curtis Anderson of The Register-Guard.

"To give anything less than your best is to sacrifice the Gift."—Steve Prefontaine

started in their season, and just as they were reaching their prime in July and August, Pre was getting tired. Often he was leading the races and he just didn't have it at the end."

"If you could put his level of fitness in April or May against the Europeans in July," Geis says, "I think it would have been a different race."

An Uncharacteristic Finish

By the second-toughest standard—the clock—Pre's month in Europe was a smashing success. He had set three American records and had been a factor in every race he ran. Yet, by that toughest of all standards—his own—Prefontaine's Summer of Europe was unsatisfactory. He returned to Eugene for six weeks of intense training to prepare for a return to Europe for a short September tour.

Once again, in private moments with close friends, he would reveal that surprising doubt in his own abilities, such a contrast to the boastful Prefontaine known to the public. Perhaps to compensate for this self-doubt, he trained ferociously and put himself in "awesome shape," in Bill Dellinger's words. "Maybe the best shape he'd ever been in."

To round into fast 5000 shape, Steve always liked to run a fast mile—blow out the tubes and work on leg speed. On a Tuesday in early September, he lined up some Oregon Track Club teammates to help pace him through a sub-4:00 mile. It was unpublicized, but this was Eugene, and a thousand people showed up to watch. This Tuesday was also a "field burning day" on which grass seed farmers in the Willamette Valley were allowed to burn the ground cover left after harvesting. An alert was broadcast, warning people with respiratory problems to stay indoors. It was not a day to run an all-out mile. But then there were those thousand fans, waiting expectantly.

Pre ran 3:58.3, and coughed blood afterward. He shrugged it off and addressed the crowd, thanking them for their support.

Shortly after, Pre left for Finland and within a week was racing in Helsinki in a 5000 against Lasse Viren. It was cold and rainy, but Steve summoned a drive on the last lap and led into the homestretch. Then, in a strategic failing that plagued him throughout his career, Pre eased off, and Viren and Garderud went by. Yet his time of 13:27.4 was pleasing, and he would have been satisfied with it except for the pain in his stomach whenever he took a deep breath.

Three nights later, Pre was in London for a two-mile race against Brendan Foster in the invitational Coca-Cola meet. Foster was becoming famous for surging a 60-second quarter in the middle of his distance races, and he was riding a hot streak. On the other hand, if there was anyone in the world who could handle such a tactic, one would think it would be Steve Prefontaine.

For five laps, Pre was there. Then Foster moved and Steve couldn't accelerate. He lost contact, and had trouble breathing. With two laps left, Pre stepped off of the track. It was the only race of his life he did not finish.

Doctors diagnosed torn muscle fibers under his rib cage, a direct result of running that mile in the smoke-filled air of Eugene. "I'll never run a race in conditions like that again," Pre vowed. "My health is more important than satisfying the people who came out. I think they would have understood if I hadn't run, but my sentiments toward them are very strong and I didn't want to let them down. I let myself down instead."

So ended Pre's European odyssey.

Reflections on Europe

The season had been a mixed success and raised as many questions as it answered. In a candid talk with Jon Hendershott of *Track & Field News*, Pre gave his own views of his summer's experiences.

"I've lost a lot of things this year, like consistency in training, eating, sleeping, and coaching, things I've always had previously. I've been very busy and so I've had to make do with what I could get. I haven't been serious in two years about running. After Munich, I've just been going through the motions.

"I think running down Frank Shorter in the three at Eugene gave me a false impression of how ready I was. I wasn't that ready, but I still felt fantastic. When he passed me, I was in a daze and it wasn't until about 280 left that I thought, 'Sheeit, if I don't get going, I'm gonna lose!' The next thing I remember is starting to lift with about 180 to go and catching Frank within 15 yards—and he wasn't slowing down either. But now I know it was strength that enabled me to do that.

"Actually, I was very pleased overall with my trips. I know if I had a little more preparation, I would have done much better. I was as ready as I could be under the circumstances. I wasn't ready to run those fast times, so I should have run the 10,000. But I thought I could run a good 5000 and I wanted to meet the best guys at their distance.

"To some extent, what the critics have said is true [about running better in Eugene], but everybody's tougher at home. At Eugene I'm the toughest I'll ever be, but it's an adjustment in Europe. It's true, I'm not as tough over there. I want to bring some top Europeans to Eugene and then we all could see how tough I could be.

"How tough in fact is Steve Prefontaine? When he's ready, very tough. When he's not ready, not very. Well, tougher than average anytime. It's just a matter of priorities, how tough you want to be. The toughness comes from my training and with the proper training I'm very tough, at home or away from home. My toughness is in my ability, when I want to win, to go out and do it. But right now I'm evaluating how much I want it.

"Actually, I ultimately would like to retire and be able to say I accomplished the things I wanted. I really don't know what those things are yet; maybe when I've achieved them, I'll know. I might wake up some day and say, 'That's enough, I've done what I wanted to do.' Planning and setting goals puts a lot of pressure on you, so I'd just as soon not plan right now.

"I don't know if Montreal is worth it. That's a decision I'm going to have to make in the next month or two. I don't know if I want to make the personal sacrifices. There's a monetary sacrifice, too. I'm tired of being a poor man.

"I was very pleased with the race," he said of his 10,000 American record in April 1974. "I think if I'm still running in future years, that will be my direction. Sure I've thought about moving up, but I don't want to run many of 'em. It's a good race but it's so damn long. I still haven't accustomed myself mentally to running 25 laps. Even though my 5000 times haven't come down drastically in the last few years, I still think I'm capable of running fast in it. I think I could have run 13:15 this year; that 13:27 in the cold at Helsinki is probably worth 10 seconds faster. I was really ready but didn't get the breaks. That's life and track though; you work hard for just a few chances."

Ralph Mann tells a story about how he used to kid Pre that he would take one more beating in the 5000 at Montreal and then win the 10,000 at Moscow in 1980. "He'd get extremely upset with me. Not with the fact that I'd said that he'd lose at Montreal, but with the fact that he'd have to go to the 10,000 and have to go to Russia to do it, and have to wait four more years."

10

The Last Season

The beginning of 1975 was still a sorting out period for Pre. The tough decision about turning pro or going for another Olympics was largely behind him. He was reconciled for the moment to at least two more years of relative poverty. At 24, he looked for an even stronger European season than in 1974, before gearing up for the Montreal Olympics.

In January 1975, Pre accepted an invitation to come to the Institute for Aerobics Research in Dallas to undergo a series of tests in what was then the nascent field of elite sports physiology. A veritable who's who of U.S. distance running came to be poked, prodded, and analyzed. Frank Shorter was there. So were Don Kardong and Kenny Moore. And Paul Geis and Jeff Galloway, an Olympic marathoner, and others. Some of the athletes viewed the various tests as a competition. Pre very definitely did.

First, he surprised the researchers on the psychological test by stating that his goal in a race was not necessarily to win but "to see who has the most guts." He then set out to prove that in the physiological testing.

Of all the procedures to measure running efficiency, lactate levels, and other indicators, none was approached with more aggression by Steve than the test for maximal oxygen capacity, "the VO_2 max test." This indicator measures the greatest volume of oxygen that can be dispatched to the muscles during exercise and was considered by some researchers to be the most promising method of identifying athletes with the potential to be the best in the world. A score in the high 70s would place the runner among the world's elite; a score in the low 80s had only been achieved at the time by a few Olympic cross country skiers and other elite endurance competitors. Everyone wanted to do well, but none more than Pre.

"When he was on that treadmill with the mask over his mouth, fire came into his eyes," Doug Brown remembers. "He knew how long everybody had gone on the treadmill, and he was just determined to go longer than anybody else. He wasn't even aware that anybody else was in the room." Pre's score of 84-plus had only been bettered by one or two athletes in the world.

"That test was more a test of will, more than anything," says Frank Shorter, who was discovered to be the most efficient runner on record during the three-day study. "I think Steve was smart enough to realize that it put him in the 99th percentile, with a whole bunch of other people. You still have to be better prepared than the people who are in the same percentile as you."

Ups and Downs

Pre returned from Dallas and went straight into the indoor season. His strength seemed greater than ever. At the CYO meet, he took second in the mile behind Marty Liquori in 3:58.6, accomplished with no speedwork whatever. But he was having trouble with a persistent sinus condition, and occasional twinges of his past sciatic problem. Pre was far from confident in February as he came to the *Los Angeles Times* Indoor meet to run a mile against world-record holder Filbert Bayi of Tanzania and John Walker of New Zealand.

The morning of the race, he went for his usual two to four miles at six-minute pace and returned complaining of a lack of zip. It would be an interesting race, he said, his first indoor one against Bayi, and his first against a front-runner of equal reputation with himself. One thing was certain—neither he nor Bayi would hang back to wait for the kick.

The tension was evident as the introductions were made. Pre looked grim. At the gun, he fought for and got the lead, passing the first quarter in 61.6 and the half in a slow 2:02.3. Something was wrong; Pre lacked his usual mid-race drive. Bayi went by, and though Pre made one more rush at the leaders with two laps left, it was obvious that he had come to the end of his run. Walker and the others passed by him, and Pre finished fifth and last in 4:03.4, his worst indoor placing since high school.

Afterward, Pre tried to be philosophical about the loss— he hadn't felt well and he hadn't done the speedwork. But he felt chagrined about his showing, especially as sportswriter John Hall had predicted he would finish ahead of Bayi in the race.

"A few days later," Hall wrote, "a letter arrived, post- marked in Eugene, with Prefontaine's bold scrawl in red ink on the envelope and his name in the top left corner. How nice, I figured, he's writing to say thanks for the column or maybe to explain what happened in the race. So I tore it open to get the good words. Out tumbled a clipping of my fum- bling forecast with this note attached:

"'Hi John: Next time, leave the predictions to experts, you ignorant ass. Steve Prefontaine.'

"I laughed for a week."

Typically, Pre came back tougher than before. The next week, he raced at his distance again, a two-mile against John Ngeno at the San Diego indoor. He continued to be bothered by minor physical problems but got a mental boost by reading that he had been voted the most popular track athlete by the readers of *Track & Field News*. As he sat reading the story on the bus taking him from the hotel to the indoor arena, he expressed genuine surprise that he was so loved. Maybe in Oregon, he said, but not all over the United States.

After a perfunctory warm-up, Pre came to the line, and only there did his lethargy leave him. He took off at the gun, and through a mile in 4:11.0, was still on his own American- record pace. The Kenyan was tucked in behind, looking fresh. With only a quarter to go, Ngeno spurted into the lead, and Pre held a visible debate with himself before dropping in behind. He waited until there was just one lap to go before unleashing perhaps the fastest last 160 yards he ever ran in an indoor race. His time was 8:24.4, not a record, but satisfying nonetheless.

"I really misjudged myself," he explained. "I could have run the last 600 yards at that pace. I felt very, very strong the last 300—very powerful, like my old self. I wanted to make my last race of the indoor season a good one, and that's what I did."

Mountain Training

To be "better prepared," in Frank Shorter's words, than the other runners in that 99th percentile, Pre accepted Frank's invitation in April to come to Denver and experiment with high-altitude training. Both athletes felt that this was the only alternative to less ethical means of enhancing performance, such as "blood doping." This process involves the extraction of an athlete's own blood during the training period, then its reinfusion at a specified time before targeted races, thus boosting the athlete's oxygen-carrying capacity. Shorter and Pre knew that with a lot of hard work, high-altitude training could accomplish the same result, as the Kenyans were later to prove. "You could look to see what the Scandinavians were doing and make that choice," Shorter recalls, "or look to see what the Kenyans were doing, and make that choice. It was pretty cut-and-dried."

Pre drove his van to Denver, then he and Frank went to Taos, New Mexico, for a week of training between 9,000 and 10,000 feet. "This was up and down a road in a ski valley, never really on a flat, and we were probably doing 15 to 16 miles a day up there," Shorter recalls. To relax, Steve tried downhill skiing, and he gradually got so he could turn both ways. "He sort of learned by force of will," Shorter chuckles. Mostly, however, they trained hard. "You're running, eating, sleeping, watching television, going to movies. That was about it. So did we socialize? Yeah, as much as you can when you're not sleeping!"

Over the three weeks they trained together, Pre was able to put the last vestiges of his distrust of Shorter to rest. From feelings "bordering almost on hate," as one friend put it, after Shorter beat him in the 1970 AAU three-mile, Pre was able to view his rival as friend. He could even write that Frank was "leaving me in the dust" on their runs at 9,200 feet. Shorter remembers one run in particular.

"We were running down this road from about 9,000 feet, and the wind was blowing up the hill so hard that you actually had to make an effort to run down the hill. It was 32 degrees, and blowing "corn snow," which is an interesting kind of snow where it has melted and then frozen again. And this pelting corn snow was hitting us and what happens is, as it hits you, it melts. So we were running down this road with this wind blowing up in our faces and I've got Pre all dressed up in ski goggles, mittens, and stuff.

"And Steve was a chronic complainer anyway. He complained under the best of conditions. He was really off on a jag: What am I doing here, what is this crap? Finally, I turned to him and said, 'Steve, you know, nobody in the world is training harder than we are right now.' It was the only time I ever ran with him that he shut up. For the rest of the run, he didn't say a word, not a word."

Only a friend and runner Pre respected could have gotten away with that.

Bringing Europe to Oregon

In the next months, the project that consumed Pre's time and energy was a tour by a team of Finnish athletes. For five years, Steve had gone to Europe each summer and seen how even small towns in Scandinavia could put on international track meets, attracting the world's top stars. He thought something similar could be started in Oregon and the Northwest, though not on the scale of the European tour. After extensive dealings with the AAU, he succeeded in arranging a five-meet tour for a small group of Finns, notably Lasse Viren.

This was what Prefontaine and his fans had been waiting for—a race against top competition in Oregon in May. Pre started to whip himself into shape. At the Oregon Twilight meet in April, he turned out for his second 10,000, this one in windy, strength-sapping weather.

"I'm sure not going to bust my ass in this crappy weather," he said bluntly before the race. He then went out and ran 28:09.4, a world-class time.

"I'm strong and my fitness is coming along at a very fast pace," a pleased Pre said after his victory laps. "I'm extremely happy with my conditioning."

Days after that race, it was announced that Viren would not be coming after all because of an injury that precluded him from racing until summer.

"Losing him makes everything I've done worthless," Pre said, with a trace of bitterness. "He was going to justify all the work. But I understand. There were meets in Europe when I didn't show up to run against him."

Despite this major disappointment, Pre continued to work hard on making the arrangements. The responsibility was a heavy one, and it added to the maturing effect on Steve, as his friend Geoff Hollister wryly remembers.

"He could now sit still for 60 seconds instead of 30, and he started packing a briefcase as his tool for organization. It looked pretty good, too, until he opened it. He started making lists and organized his days better. He had so many irons in the fire, how he kept track of things is beyond me.

"Steve really needed help with the Finnish tour. The AAU had him so messed up with their belated approval that many details had been overlooked. I looked over his list and asked, 'How are you going to pick them up at the airport?'

"'I don't know.'

"'Well, how many pole vault poles do you think Antti Kalliomaki has? You going to show up in your MG?'

"'Damn it, then you do it!'

"For Steve, that was progress—a year earlier, the Finns would have been greeted by a smile and two seats. He was learning to delegate."

Without Viren, Pre had no one to run against. The hassles of the tour had occupied his mental energies, but now he was finally able to think about going for some records.

The second meet on the itinerary was in his hometown of Coos Bay; the race was 2000 meters. Despite the chilly evening, a crowd of 4,000 showed up in Pirate Stadium to see their native son. Oregon teammate Dave Taylor was there.

"Pre came up to us two hours before the race and asked if anyone knew what the American record for 2000 meters was, as if he didn't know. And he says he thinks he'll try for the American record. I seriously thought he was joking, because this had to be one of the most low-key meets I've ever been to in my life."

Lars Kaupang led the first two laps in 2:02.0 before Prefontaine took over and pushed through two more 60-second laps. He finished with a 59.4 for a new American record of 5:01.4.

"He said he would do it and he did it," Taylor marvels. "I mean, he's on the track in Coos Bay at 10 o'clock one night with 200 loggers in the stands, and he does it."

For the next 30 minutes, Pre signed programs for the hundreds of Coos Bay kids who had chanted "Go Pre! Go Pre!" every time their hero passed by the Pirate grandstands. They continued to cluster around him as he did his warm-down, like puppies after mother's milk. Perhaps it was here, in Coos Bay, at home, where one saw the full impact that Pre the Legend had upon the young people of Oregon.

Speaking Out

Even while he was making news on the track, Pre was making more news off of it. He had been embarrassed and chagrined when the wire services had taken a quote of his out of context in a story about the inadequacies of the American amateur system. Every four years, Pre had said, the United States expected its athletes to win medals at the Olympic Games but then forgot about them for the three years in between.

"People say I should be running for a gold medal, for the old red, white, and blue and all that bull," he had said in April. "But it's not going to be that way. I'm the one who has made all the sacrifices. Those are my American records, not my country's." This became known as his "To hell with love of country" speech, and while Pre regretted being thought of as unpatriotic, he didn't take back his words. He didn't live his life based on opinion polls.

That furor slowly quieted, but Pre was never one to back down from conflict. He had always had the strength of his convictions, and combined with his bluntness was an awareness that he had a special role to play in how the sport was perceived and how it was administered.

Now the AAU was imposing a moratorium on competition by athletes a certain number of days before and after its own international dual meets. The goal was to force the athletes to pass up the important European invitationals and instead compete on the AAU tour. Pre's decision to skip the 1974 AAU Championships, and the international meets held subsequently, had produced a punitive response from an organization not used to being ignored. Pre was fed up.

"If they don't let me go and run where I want this summer," Pre threatened, "then I just may not compete in the AAU event here [in Eugene]." The subject of the AAU reminded Steve of his biggest gripe.

"I've got bills to pay," he explained to George Pasero of the *Oregon Journal*. "I'm just like any other American. If I don't pay my electric bill, they turn off my lights. After college, our athletes are turned out to pasture. We have no Olympic program in this country. It's as simple as that. No sports medicine, no camps, no nothing. I'm not talking about subsidizing us. I'm just talking about a national plan. I want to see some interest from somebody. In the past, we've sat back and let our natural talent do it. Well, the rest of the world has caught up."

"I'm really not trying to get under anybody's skin," Pre had said at another time in a less strident tone. "I'm just trying to bring the problems to a head and an understanding. To make the people of this country realize what's happening is that the amateurs do not have the same benefits as, say, the Europeans. And I'd just like to bring this to the acknowledgment of the public."

As the last race on the tour approached, a 5000 meters—in Eugene, of course—Pre was justifiably proud of the tour he had organized. Despite the AAU and Viren's pullout, the meets had been a success.

"Nobody believed I could pull it off," Pre said to Leo Davis of *The Oregonian* during the last week in May. "I couldn't have done it without help, but from the beginning, it has been my responsibility. I carried the load. I like what has happened. I just couldn't afford to do it again the same way.

"I'm in for quite a bit. With luck I get back the expenses, but I can't get anything for the hours of work. As an amateur, I've gotten used to working without pay. If I had been paid 50 cents an hour for every workout and every race, I'd be rich enough to sponsor tours."

One of these days, Davis observed, "an athlete, maybe Pre, will strike the spark that unites track and field and brings the AAU to its creaky knees. United, athletes have that much clout; without them there is no AAU."

"It's time for a change," concluded the column, which appeared on May 27. "Even Pre can't run forever."

The Last Race

Pre had hoped that the 5000 on May 29 would be the climactic race in a duel between himself and Lasse Viren. With Viren out, Pre called upon Frank Shorter to step down to the 5-K distance for this meet. Shorter, who had been visiting and training in Eugene, willingly agreed.

The race itself was not a typical Prefontaine race. He followed Frank through an 8:40.5 two-mile, and led only laps 5 and 6. Then, with three laps to go, he accelerated to 63-second pace. The 7,000 spectators in the stands reacted vocally, almost with relief that Pre still had that spark at Eugene, that winning streak at Hayward Field. He finished with a 60.3 last lap and a winning time of 13:23.8, just 1.9 seconds off his own American record, in his first serious 5000 of 1975. His winning string at distances over a mile in Eugene was extended to 25 straight. He never lost.

"I'm ahead of what I've been in the past when it comes to strength, but not fitness," Steve assessed after his warm-down jog. "I need one fast race. I always run better after a good mile, and I think I'm capable of one next week. If I get a good mile, I should have a good summer."

11

Final Lap

Against the unbearableness that was felt at the time of Steve Prefontaine's death, it was comforting to know that virtually everyone he cared about was close to him on the last night of his life.

His last race over, Pre took several victory laps, saying thanks to the people of Eugene. At one point, he stopped and talked with his family who had come from Coos Bay to watch the meet. After signing autographs, he went to the apartment of his friend Mark Feig to shower.

Later, Pre stopped by the University of Oregon track-and-field awards banquet and talked to Bill Dellinger about his training. After a brief visit, he and his girlfriend, Nancy Alleman, left for the Paddock Tavern where he socialized and had several glasses of beer. After about an hour, they left for the party being held at Geoff Hollister's house to celebrate the end of the Finnish tour and arrived about 10:00 P.M.

Shorter, Kenny Moore, and the Finns were there. Pre's parents, Ray and Elfriede, were also there, as was high school coach Walt McClure. Pre was happy and relieved that the tour was over. According to the guests in attendance, he drank about four or five beers in the two hours he remained at the party. Pre spent his time there visiting with family and friends. He didn't appear drunk to those present.

At 12:15 A.M., Pre left with Nancy and Frank. "We all three got into the MG and drove down to the University of Oregon ticket office where Nancy had left her car and let her

151

off," Shorter told Jerry Uhrhammer of Eugene's *The Register-Guard*. "Then he drove me home."

Shorter was staying with Kenny Moore at his home on one of the hills encircling Eugene. He and Pre sat in the car for a few minutes, discussing what their stand would be on the Amateur Athletic Union (AAU) moratorium. Both agreed that they would not duck the championship meet but would run their specialties all out and then take on the AAU. With that, Shorter got out of the car, and Pre drove down the hill.

The Accident

What exactly happened at the bottom of Skyline Boulevard is open to question. It was a road Pre had run along dozens of times in his years in Eugene. As it approaches its intersection with Birch Lane, there is a sharp curve. Although there was no indication of excessive speed, Pre's 1973 MGB crossed the center line, went over the curb, and hit one wall of the natural rock that lines either side of the street. His car flipped over, pinning him underneath. The MGB was equipped with a roll bar, but Pre was not wearing his seat belt at the time of the accident.

The house closest to the accident was owned by the Alvarado family. Bill and Karen Alvarado had gone to the track meet, then visited friends, before returning home shortly after midnight. They made sandwiches and sat with the windows open on the stuffy night. The Alvarados recalled what happened next in a 1985 article by Cathy Henkel of *The Register-Guard*.

> As they ate and talked, their ears perked at the loud intruding engine of a sports car on the road just below their bedroom windows. Then they heard the screech of tires, the "thunk" of impact, and silence. "Absolute, dead silence," she remembered. "It was so absolutely still that we knew something was wrong."
>
> Bill Alvarado decided to see what had happened. Within seconds, he was out the door and on the narrow, wooded road. He saw nothing at first, then heard

a car starting around the curve and was momentarily blinded when its headlights flashed into his eyes.

"I thought he'd hit the stop sign," Alvarado recalled. "I stood right in the street and waved my arms. But there was no way he was going to stop and I had to get out of the way in a hurry." Alvarado jumped aside as a light-colored MGB raced by him. Angry, he hopped into his Jeep and tried to follow, but the car quickly vanished around the turn. Alvarado looped around Hendricks Park, and when he turned off Birch and onto Skyline, he saw the wreck of another MGB. He parked, yelled to his wife that someone was hurt and to call for help while he returned to the overturned car. Ten years later in retelling the story, he is still chilled when he remembers what happened next.

"I didn't know who it was, but he was still gasping and somehow I managed to lift the car part of the way off him. But that's all I could do. I couldn't get the car completely off and I couldn't pull him out.

"I'm not a medical person but I know he was still breathing. If I could have had help lifting the car, if that other car had stopped, we could have saved time and maybe together we could have lifted it off him."

When Alvarado could no longer hold the car up, he ran to get help. While he was gone, the Eugene police arrived, but by that time, Pre was dead.

After hearing Bill Alvarado's story, the police tracked down the 20-year-old driver of the other MGB. He said that he had arrived on the scene after the accident, and upon seeing someone pinned underneath the overturned auto, panicked and sped off to get his father, a doctor. The driver said that he could tell the driver had been injured but not whether he was still alive. A week after the accident, the police reported that the driver had passed a lie-detector test, and the case was closed.

Later that Friday morning, a sample of Pre's blood was taken by the mortician at the behest of the police, a procedure the Lane County medical examiner at the time, Dr. Ed Wilson, called "not standard."

"The medical examiner is the one who does that," Wilson said. "All I can say is that this was done in an unusual manner and I don't remember ever having it happen that way before or since. I was very angry about it."

The deviation in procedure is an important point to Prefontaine's family and friends. Depending on how and from where the blood was taken, the test can be off by as much as 20 percent. No one disputes that Pre had been drinking beer that evening, or condones drinking and driving, but none of the guests at the party thought him to be too impaired to drive. "He was in the same condition I was in," Shorter said. "We'd had three or four beers and he seemed fine. I trusted him to drive."

The mortician's sample recorded the level of alcohol in Pre's blood at 0.16 percent, well above the Oregon legal limit of 0.10 percent. To some, it was a clear case of a single-car accident caused by driving while intoxicated. Perhaps Pre's driving was affected enough that he simply misjudged the curve and his approach speed. Perhaps, as one policeman speculated, he was reaching for a cassette tape and took his eyes off the road. Perhaps he failed to make the turn for an altogether different reason.

The result is the same.

"The Magic Was Gone Forever"

The next day, a Friday, was quieter than usual, as the people of Eugene awoke to the mind-numbing news that Steve Prefontaine was dead. Many who read or listened to that mournful statement had watched Pre at the peak of his vitality 15 hours before, sweeping around the last bend of the Hayward Field track, heading for the finish tape. Now he was gone.

Parents groped vainly for a way to tell children who had run after Pre for autographs the day before that their idol was dead. It was difficult enough for adults to comprehend.

Soon the eulogies would come pouring in to newspapers, television stations, the University of Oregon athletic depart-

On Pre: Frank Shorter

[The AAU] was what we were discussing the night he died, sitting in the car. I think it was only natural for me to go on with the fight, and I felt a certain obligation to do it. That was one of the many reasons I did it, but it did have an influence. There's a certain aspect of any athlete's mentality, which is to not waste an effort. There was this feeling you didn't want to waste or squander any effort Pre put forward. In other words, if you could do something to keep that momentum going, then you should do it.

[Pre's death] is still a "shock" kind of feeling. For me, it was my first dose of reality involving death, where I could be with someone one moment, and the next moment they're dead. It was the first time for me involving a friend. It had impact, and it still does. It's one of those feelings that kind of never goes away.

Frank Shorter won the gold medal in the 1972 Olympic Marathon and the silver medal in the 1976 Olympic Marathon.

ment, and the Prefontaine family. Plans were made for memorial services in Eugene and Coos Bay, with burial in his hometown. It was all so swift and final.

Friday night, a group of about a dozen of Pre's friends gathered at Kenny Moore's house. In the conversation that followed, the participants learned that few of them felt themselves to have been intimate friends of Pre's, according to one who was there. The reason: "Nobody could keep up with him."

The elemental fact was that Steve knew and was friends with a great many people of widely varying backgrounds and interests—from Coos Bay toughs to college professors. He was constantly surprising those who thought they knew him by the scope of his projects, most of them unpublicized. Many in attendance that night were startled to learn that Pre had started a running club at the state prison in Salem, Oregon, and had made regular visits there for several years to provide workout schedules and encouragement.

Pre would astonish those who thought of him as a jock with his knowledge of art, cars, photography, and carpentry. He was constantly on the go, visiting both track and nontrack friends all around Eugene.

"He never liked to be by himself," says a friend who was closer than all but a few. "Scared to be by himself. I don't know why I'm saying that, but I think it's true. He didn't like to be alone."

In early June 1975, it was Pre's People who felt alone. The grief was perhaps best expressed in a letter of condolence Oregon's legendary governor at the time, Tom McCall, typed on the Sunday after the accident.

"Dear Mr. and Mrs. Prefontaine: Oregon has never been struck such a tragic blow. Pre was an essential part of the pride we all feel in Oregon. He was a magnificent performer and a human being of admirable independence. No one so young has ever made such an imprint on our state, the nation, and the world—at least no one from this part of the country. Nor will we see his like again in my lifetime. . . . These are just words and I could go on wringing my hands, but they are words that struggle to say to you how we all feel in this moment of deprivation. . . ."

Steve Prefontaine's funeral was held in Pirate Stadium, inside the track he ran around so many times during his high school years. He was buried at a cemetery in Coos Bay, dressed in his Olympic uniform. His pallbearers, appropriately, were all runners, dressed in national team warm-up suits. At a memorial service the next evening at Hayward Field in Eugene, Kenny Moore gave the eulogy, and other athletes and friends put words to their emotions. As they spoke, the scoreboard clock continued to run, until it was stopped at 12:36.0, a time Pre once said he would be satisfied with in the three-mile. During the last minute, the crowd of 4,000 stood and cheered, and many present still maintain the sun broke through the clouds as the clock stopped, just as it had whenever Pre had stepped onto the track. Then it was over, and the people filed silently out of the stands. They had cheered for the last time for Pre at Hayward Field.

For Pre's People, a unique and personal relationship died that night in the spring of 1975. "It's hard for some people, even here in Eugene, to understand the bond between Pre and his fans," one of Pre's admirers wrote. "It was hard to understand, and hard to explain, unless you experienced it."

Other great athletes have made Eugene their home in the intervening decades. Alberto Salazar, Rudy Chapa, Mary Slaney, Joaquim Cruz, and many others have raced at Hayward Field in front of the knowledgeable, supportive hometown fans.

But there will never be another Pre. Never be another athlete possessing the charisma, fearlessness, the warmth of Steve Prefontaine. Never another athlete with sufficient energy to start a jogging club, tutor teenagers, organize tours, or work for the parole of a prison inmate.

An old rival, whose high school two-mile record Pre broke, expressed the mood of a Eugene without Pre a year after his death. For those who saw Prefontaine run, it is a mood that lasts to this day.

"It seemed," said Rick Riley, "that those of us running in the meet were only minor performers and that any minute the Star would appear and the crowds would roar to life, athlete and spectator giving and taking whatever it is that each needs and wants. I stood there on the track near the finish but he did not appear. The magic was gone forever."

12

Pre's Legacy

"To give anything less than your best is to sacrifice the Gift."

When Pre would speak as he often did to young athletes at clinics and camps, he would end his talk with this sentence. For him, the Gift was running, which had taken him from junior high benchwarmer to the cover of *Sports Illustrated* by the time he was 18. For him, the gift was not something handed to one, but something that had to be pursued with tenacity and diligence. Pre acknowledged that he was a good runner, could even become in time the best in the world, but he sincerely believed that many others had been born with more running talent than he; that everything achieved had been due to hard work and always giving his best. "It made him mad to see wasted talent," a close friend remembers.

Pre could be incredibly eloquent at times, and quite profane at others. Much of both came out of his honesty. Leave it to Steve to talk to junior high school students without embarrassment about the dangers of venereal disease. Or while in high school to respond to a question about military plans for the future with "stay out as long as I can, don't believe in the war."

It was his honesty and don't-mess-with-me attitude that inevitably brought him afoul of the Amateur Athletic Union. While proclaiming that he was "not really trying to get under anyone's skin," he proceeded to do just that. Other athletes had complained about the restrictions and sanctions placed upon them by the bureaucracy. Pre sank his teeth in and wouldn't let go. His example in life and the profound shock of his death increased the resolve of many to carry on the fight.

In 1978, the U.S. Congress, after hearing testimony from Frank Shorter and athletes from other sports, passed the Amateur Sports Act, in effect breaking the stranglehold of the AAU and reorganizing a number of sports, including track and field. In 1981, the Association of Road Racing Athletes challenged the rules of international amateurism by offering prize money openly to the top finishers in the Cascade Run-Off in Portland, Oregon, Pre's backyard. Slowly at first, and then with increasing velocity, "shamateurism," with its under-the-table payments and hypocrisy, gave way to direct payments to athletes in both road running and track and field.

Just as Pre served as a catalyst for dramatic change in the organization of the sport, he helped give personality to the young company that grew into Nike. He was the first athlete to be paid to wear Nike shoes. He was the first person in the company to try to get top international athletes to wear the new brand. His method was to send a personal letter and some free shoes to his top rivals, asking them to give the shoes a try. Bill Rodgers and Mary Slaney, Olympic medalists John Walker, Rod Dixon, Brendan Foster, and Dick Quax all received shoes from Pre and ended up wearing Nikes at some point in their careers. Pre styled himself as "National Public Relations Manager," but he was really Nike's first sports marketing agent. "Basically, Steve showed us how to do it," says Geoff Hollister, who took over for Pre after his death. "We look back and credit him with being the first sports marketing guy we had. Our world at the time was what was going on in Eugene. Steve, he's talking to people all over the world, and that was a whole different attitude."

Today, at the Nike corporate headquarters in Beaverton, Oregon, there stands in the middle of the campus the Prefontaine Building, with a statue of Pre facing the foyer. With all of the hundreds of superstars from various sports who have been in the Nike fold, Pre is the only one to have been accorded such an honor.

On Pre: Steve Prefontaine

> Some people create with words, or with music, or
> with a brush and paints. I like to make something beau-
> tiful when I run. I like to make people stop and say,
> "I've never seen anyone run like that before." It's more
> than just a race, it's style. It's doing something better
> than anyone else. It's being creative.

There are other tributes to Pre's memory. The annual
Prefontaine Classic in Eugene has evolved into the best invitational track meet in the United States, and one of the best
in the world. Sellout crowds and national television coverage
have been hallmarks of recent editions of the meet. In
September of each year, the Prefontaine Memorial 10-K is
held in Coos Bay along a route Pre used to train over often. A
monument listing his accomplishments stands in a prominent
place along the waterfront promenade in his hometown. In
Eugene, the wood-chip jogging trail in Alton Baker Park that
Pre lobbied for unsuccessfully in his life was approved the day
after his death; instead of the one-mile circuit envisioned by
Pre and the Decathlon Club, however, five miles of trails were
constructed and are used by runners every day of the year.

In the two decades after Pre's death, his athletic contemporaries have gone on to further fame on the track and off.
Pre's college teammate Mac Wilkins won the Olympic discus
gold medal in 1976 and set the world record that Pre had felt
would be his one day. Lasse Viren of Finland repeated as the
gold medalist in the 5000- and 10,000-meter races and finished fifth in the marathon in Montreal, again appearing
nearly invincible after several years of mediocrity. Oregon
head track coach Bill Bowerman continued his experimenta-
tion with shoe design and co-founded Nike, which grew into
the largest sports-related corporation in the world. From
1973, Bill Dellinger remained as the head coach at Oregon
for more than 20 years, guiding Alberto Salazar, Rudy Chapa,
and dozens of other distance runners to national champi-

onships and Olympic team berths. Mary Slaney grew up to set extraordinary world and American records during a tumultuous career spanning three decades. Oregon teammate and rival Paul Geis made the final of the Olympic 5000 in Montreal but never reached the level expected of the "next Pre," as he was unfairly tagged. Roommate and friend Pat Tyson became a high school coach in Spokane, Washington, and mentored his teams to a score of state championships in track and cross country. University of Oregon runners Dave Taylor and Geoff Hollister became senior executives at Nike in Beaverton, Oregon. Frank Shorter went on to win the silver medal in the marathon in Montreal, and became one of the icons of the running boom. Don Kardong finished fourth in the 1976 Olympic Marathon and, through his subsequent efforts as a road racing administrator, helped end the era of "shamateurism." All were touched in an ongoing way by the life and death of Steve Prefontaine, as were Pre's People.

Twenty years after he established a running club in the state penitentiary, the club still exists, with 125 members. Each year, they run a 5-K in Steve's memory within the walls, but open to runners from the outside. The sobering fact is that some of the convicts participating are the same ones Pre wrote training schedules for two decades earlier. They felt he was one of them, a maverick.

For the rest of Pre's People, he is kept alive in memory. Some still make a pilgrimage to the scene of the crash, now called Pre's Rock, to leave flowers or a running medal, or just to see the "5-30-75" on the rock wall, first painted there 20 years ago, and faithfully renewed by unknown persons in the years since.

Others run on the trail named for him, or watch the international track meet held in his honor each year. All of them recognize that Pre's legacy will endure as long as he is remembered, rounding that last turn at Hayward Field and heading for the finish line, eyes on the clock, ready to break the tape one more time.

Appendix

Outdoor Track Racing Career

DATE	MEET	SITE	EVENT	TIME	PLACE	COMMENTS
1967						
3/25	Indian Club Relays	Roseburg	Mile	4:31.8	2nd	
4/1	v Grants Pass		Mile	4:32.0	1st	
4/4	v Reedsport	Reedsport	2M	9:42.1	1st	
4/7	Spike Leslie Relays	North Bend	DMR*	4:32.1r	1st	
4/15	v Roseburg		880	2:03.5	1st	
4/15	v Roseburg		Mile	4:48.9	1st	tie
4/21			Mile	4:32.2	2nd	
4/28			2M	9:46.2	1st	
5/2	v Reedsport	Coos Bay	880	2:09.5	3rd	
5/5	County	Coos Bay	Mile	4:36.3	1st	
5/11	SCJV	Coos Bay	Mile	4:29.1	1st	
5/11	SCJV	Coos Bay	880	2:06.3	1st	
5/18	District	Springfield	2M	9:52.3	4th	
1968						
3/23	Indian Club Relays	Roseburg	Mile	4:13.8	1st	
3/29	v Grants Pass	Grants Pass	2M	9:13.9	1st	
4/5	Spike Leslie Relays	North Bend	DMR	4:21.1r	1st	
4/12	v Roseburg	Roseburg	880	1:57.2	1st	
4/12	v Roseburg	Roseburg	Mile	4:51.8	1st	
4/19	v Springfield-N Eugene	Coos Bay	Mile	4:23.4	1st	
4/26	Corvallis Invitational	Corvallis	2M	9:01.3	1st	state record
5/3	Coos County	Coos Bay	Mile	4:14.1	1st	
5/10	v North Bend	Coos Bay	880	1:56.2	1st	
5/17	District	Springfield	2M	9:13.2	1st	
5/24	State Meet	Corvallis	2M	9:02.7	1st	

*Distance medley relay

Date	Meet	Site	Event	Time	Place	Comments
1969						
3/29	Indian Club Relays	Roseburg	DMR	4:12.6r	1st	
3/29	Indian Club Relays	Roseburg	SpMR*	1:56.4r	1st	
4/5	v Grants Pass	Coos Bay	Mile	4:11.1	1st	
4/5	v Grants Pass	Coos Bay	2M	9:13.4	1st	
4/11	v Roseburg	Coos Bay	Mile	4:19.4	1st	
4/11	v Roseburg	Coos Bay	880	1:54.3	1st	
4/11	v Roseburg	Coos Bay	MileR	51.5r	1st	
4/18	v South Eugene	Coos Bay	Mile	4:21.1	1st	
4/18	v South Eugene	Coos Bay	880	1:57.7	1st	
4/18	v South Eugene	Coos Bay	MileR	52.6r	1st	
4/25	Corvallis Invitational	Corvallis	2M	8:41.5	1st	national HS† record
5/2	v Springfield	Springfield	440	53.5	1st	
5/9	Coos County	Coos Bay	Mile	4:06.9	1st	
5/16	v North Bend	North Bend	Mile	4:22.4	1st	
5/23	District	Springfield	Mile	4:07.4	1st	
5/23	District	Springfield	2M	9:14.3	1st	
5/30	State Meet	Corvallis	Mile	4:08.4	1st	
5/30	State Meet	Corvallis	2M	9:03.0	1st	
6/14	Golden West Invitational	Sacramento	Mile	4:06.0	1st	#10 all-time HS
6/29	AAU Championships	Miami	3M	13:43.0	4th	#3 all-time HS
7/12	Hawaii Invitational	Honolulu	2M	8:48.8	2nd	Lindgren 8:45.6
7/19	US v USSR	Los Angeles	5000	14:40.0	5th	
7/31	US v Europe	Stuttgart	5000	13:52.8	3rd	
8/5	US v W. Germany	Augsburg	5000	14:07.4	2nd	
8/13	US v Great Britain	London	5000	14:38.4	4th	
1970						
3/21	v Fresno St., Stanford	Fresno	2M	8:40.0	1st	
3/28	v Texas, El Paso	El Paso	3M	13:48.8	1st	
4/4	v Washington	Seattle	Mile	4:03.2	1st	
4/4	v Washington	Seattle	2M	8:51.6	1st	
4/11	v California	Berkeley	3M	13:30.6	1st	
4/18	v UCLA	Eugene	Mile	4:05.3	1st	tie with Divine

*Sprint medley relay   †High school

Date	Meet	Site	Event	Time	Place	Comments
4/18	v UCLA	Eugene	2M	8:46.4	1st	
4/25	v Washington State	Eugene	3M	13:12.8	1st	
5/2	v Oregon State	Eugene	Mile	4:00.4	1st	
5/9	Northern Division	Seatttle	3M	13:32.0	1st	
5/16	Pac-8 Championships	Los Angeles	3M	13:27.8	1st	
6/5	Oregon Twilight	Eugene	Mile	3:57.4	2nd	Divine 3:56.3
6/20	NCAA Championships	Des Moines	3M	13:22.0	1st	
6/26	AAU Championships	Bakersfield	3M	13:26.0	5th	Shorter 13:24.2
7/16	US v W. Germany	Stuttgart	5000	13:39.6	2nd	Norpoth 13:34.6
7/24	US v USSR	Leningrad	5000	13:49.4	2nd	
7/26	International	Moscow	1500	3:44.9	1st	
12/12	Postal	Eugene	3M	13:25.6	1st	

1971

Date	Meet	Site	Event	Time	Place	Comments
3/20	Quadrangular	Eugene	2M	8:33.2	1st	
3/27	v San Diego State	San Diego	Mile	4:00.2	1st	
4/3	v Stanford	Eugene	3M	13:01.6	1st	
4/10	v Washington	Eugene	Mile	4:02.6	1st	
4/10	v Washington	Eugene	2M	8:36.2	1st	
4/17	v California	Eugene	3M	13:34.0	1st	
4/24	v UCLA	Westwood	Mile	3:59.1	1st	
5/8	v Oregon State	Corvallis	2M	8:42.4	1st	
5/15	Northern Division	Pullman	2M	8:42.4	1st	
5/22	Pac-8 Championships	Seattle	Mile	4:01.5	1st	
5/22	Pac-8	Seattle	3M	13:18.0	1st	
6/6	Oregon Twilight	Eugene	Mile	3:57.4	2nd	Kvalheim 3:56.4
6/17	NCAA Champs. (heat)	Seattle	3M	13:34.6	1st	
6/19	NCAA Champs. (final)	Seattle	3M	13:20.2	1st	
6/25	AAU Championships	Eugene	3M	12:58.6	1st	
7/3	v USSR All Stars	Berkeley	5000	13:30.4	1st	AR*
7/16	v Africa	Durham	5000	13:57.6	1st	Yifter mistook finish
8/2	Pan Am Games	Cali	5000	13:52.6	1st	

*American record

Date	Meet	Site	Event	Time	Place	Comments
1972						
3/18	v Fresno State	Fresno	2M	8:55.4	1st	
3/25	All Comers	Bakersfield	6M	27:22.4	1st	collegiate record
4/1	Oregon Invitational	Eugene	2M	8:35.8	1st	
4/8	v Washington	Seattle	Mile	4:07.3	1st	
4/15	v Nebraska	Lincoln	2M	8:35.2	1st	
4/23	Oregon Twilight	Eugene	Mile	3:56.7	1st	10th best U.S.
4/29	v Washington State	Eugene	5000	13:29.6	1st	AR
5/6	v Oregon State	Eugene	1500	3:39.8	1st	
5/20	Pac-8 Championships	Stanford	3M	13:32.2	1st	
6/1	NCAA Champs. (heat)	Eugene	5000	14:01.4	1st	
6/3	NCAA Champs. (final)	Eugene	5000	13:31.4	1st	
6/24	Rose Festival	Gresham	3000	7:45.8	1st	AR
7/6	Olympic Trials (heat)	Eugene	5000	13:51.2	1st	
7/9	Olympic Trials (final)	Eugene	5000	13:22.8	1st	AR, 4th best world
8/2	Bislett Games	Oslo	1500	3:39.4	2nd	Vasala 3:38.3
8/3	Bislett Games	Oslo	3000	7:44.2	1st	AR
8/24	Pre-Olympic	Munich	2M	8:19.4	1st	AR
9/7	Olympic Games (heat)	Munich	5000	13:32.6	2nd	Puttemans 13:31.8
9/10	Olympic Games (final)	Munich	5000	13:28.3	4th	Viren 13:26.4
9/13	Zauli Memorial	Rome	5000	13:26.4	2nd	Del Buono 13:22.4 NR*
9/15	Coca-Cola	London	2M	8:24.8	2nd	Dixon 8:19.4
1973						
3/17	All Comers	Eugene	2000	5:06.2	1st	
3/24	All Comers	Bakersfield	6M	27:09.4	1st	AR
3/31	Oregon Invitational	Eugene	2M	8:31.8	1st	
4/7	v Washington	Eugene	Mile	4:03.2	1st	
4/14	Quadrangular	Eugene	Mile	3:56.8	1st	59.1, 1:59.0, 2:58.4, 58.4
4/14	Quadrangular	Eugene	3M	13:06.4	1st	best ever one-day double

*National record